Russian Research Center Studies

41

THE SOVIET INDUSTRIALIZATION DEBATE, 1924-1928

THE SOVIET

INDUSTRIALIZATION

DEBATE, 1924-1928

by Alexander Erlich

HARVARD UNIVERSITY PRESS

CAMBRIDGE, MASSACHUSETTS 1960

The Russian Research Center of Harvard University is supported by a grant from the Carnegie Corporation. The Center carries out inter-disciplinary study of Russian institutions and behavior and related subjects.

This volume was prepared under a grant from the Carnegie Corporation of New York. That Corporation is not, however, the author, owner, publisher, or proprietor of this publication and is not to be understood as approving by virtue of its grant any of the statements made or views expressed herein.

To the Memory of
HENRYK ERLICH

Acknowledgments

A few brief paragraphs can only inadequately express my gratitude to all those who by their cooperation and support have made it possible for me to complete this book.

My debt is greatest to three persons. Abba P. Lerner, my chief guide in economic theory during my graduate years, suggested the general direction of this study and has followed its development with unfaltering perseverance and incisive criticism. Abram Bergson helped me to delineate the topic more sharply, and has been a source of invaluable aid and stimulation as the indomitable reader and critic of several successive drafts. Alexander Gerschenkron took an active interest in my work at an early stage and has cleared away many a hurdle by his good advice and warm encouragement. To the extent that this book represents any contribution whatsoever, a lion's share of credit must go to these men. However, neither they nor my other advisers and friends should be held responsible for the opinions expressed in it and for the many errors that undoubtedly remain.

The writing of my doctoral dissertation, which was submitted to the Graduate Faculty of the New School for Social Research in early 1953 and which forms the basis for the present study, was done under the tenure of a research fellowship of the Russian Research Center of Harvard University. Clyde Kluckhohn, the first director of the Center, was unstinting in his kindness and readiness to help. As a result, I was able to devote my full time over a period of four years to research in the problem area of this book in an atmosphere of high intellectual inspiration and good companionship. Merle Fainsod, Walter Galenson, Gregory Grossman, Donald R. Hodgman, and Barrington Moore read portions of the original manuscript, and their critical suggestions resulted in many improvements. Exchanging views with them, as well as with Miriam H. Berlin, Joseph S. Berliner, Robert V. Daniels, Alexander Eckstein, Franklyn D. Holzman, Benjamin I. Schwartz, Demitri Shimkin, Carolyn R. Shilling, and Adam B. Ulam, was a most gratifying experience.

During the same period, and in years that followed, it was my good fortune to have the comments of Eduard Heimann, Adolph Lowe, and Hans P. Neisser, my teachers at the New School for Social Research, as well as of Evsey D. Domar, James S. Duesenberry, Wassily Leontief, and P. N. Rosenstein-Rodan, all of whom consented to read particular chapters of my manuscript. Boris Nicolaevsky was very generous in lending books from his rich collection and in giving me the benefit of his reminiscences on problems and personalities. Lev Magerovsky, Curator of the Russian and Eastern European Archives at Columbia University, put me in his debt by letting me read the very interesting memoirs of N. V. Vol'ski covering the period of the twenties. The kind permission to use the Trotsky Archives of the Houghton Library of Harvard University made it possible for me to incorporate some material which had not been published before.

In the final states of my work, also, there were many who lent a helping hand: Helen W. Parsons, Administrative Assistant to the Director of the Russian Research Center displayed true virtuosity in securing required secretarial assistance at the shortest possible time and was an unfailing source of good cheer; Ruth DeWitt, Joan J. Miller, Mary E. Towle, and Rose DiBenedetto were conscientious and competent typists of successive drafts. I want to thank also the staff of the Harvard University Press; especially Eleanor D. Kewer for her understanding cooperation and Ann Orlov for editing the manuscript with great skill and care.

A research training grant from the Social Science Research Council allowed me to complete extensive preparatory work. A summer grant from the same organization, awarded in 1957, enabled me to make substantial progress toward the completion of the present manuscript, and a contribution from Columbia University's Council for Research in Social Sciences helped to defray typing expenses.

Some of the material contained in this volume has previously appeared in print. Portions of Chapters II and IX are taken from my article, "Preobrazhenski and the Economics of Soviet Industrialization" (*Quarterly Journal of Economics*, 64, February 1950). Chapter V represents, by and large, a section of my paper, "Stalin's Views on Soviet Economic Development" (in Ernest J. Simmons, ed., *Continuity and Change in Russian and Soviet Thought*, Cambridge, 1955). I am indebted to the publishers of these essays for permission to reproduce parts of them, and to the Macmillan Company for the permission to use, in slightly changed form, a diagram from Abba P. Lerner's *The Economics of Control* (New York, 1944).

Last, but very definitely not least, thanks are due to my wife and daughter for their help in proofreading and typing, and above all for their willingness to bear with an author in travail.

Alexander Erlich

March 8, 1960
The Russian Institute,
Columbia University

CONTENTS

THE SOVIET INDUSTRIALIZATION
DEBATE, 1924-1928

The following abbreviations have been used in the footnotes and in the references:

B	*Bol'shevik*
EO	*Ekonomicheskoe obozrenie* (Economic Review)
P	*Pravda*
PKh	*Planovoe khozyaistvo* (Planned Economy)
QJE	*Quarterly Journal of Economics*
VKA	*Vestnik Kommunisticheskoi akademii* (Journal of the Communist Academy)
VKP	Vsesoyuznaya Kommunisticheskaya Partiya (Communist Party of the Soviet Union)

Introduction

THE years 1924–1928 witnessed a remarkable debate in the Soviet Union. Its major participants were leading Communist theoreticians and eminent nonparty economists; the keenly interested audience included everyone who was politically and intellectually articulate in Soviet society. The debate ranged far and wide from issues concerning the theory of value to day-to-day political minutiae. At its center, overshadowing all the rest, loomed the problem of the appropriate speed and pattern for the prospective economic development of the country.

A discussion of this scope was in keeping with a time-honored tradition. In its sweep and in the dimensions of the problems it raised, it revived memories of the ideological battle royal which had reached its peak before the turn of the century when the protagonists of Westernization led by the "students of Marx" had clashed with the Populist defenders of Russia's "uniqueness." Indeed, many Soviet debaters harked back to this old dispute in search of supporting argument and polemical spice. And just as the pre-revolutionary logomachy moved towards its climax under the impact of such momentous events as the hurried industrialization of the eighties and nineties and the disintegration of the Populist movement after 1881, its Soviet sequel was born of a cycle of stunning defeats and unexpected successes. The crushing of the German Communist uprising in early 1921 and the stabilization of the mark in 1924 marked the beginning and the end of the chain of events which shattered the hopes of the imminent European revolution. At the same time, the retreat from War Communism to the NEP (New Economic Policy) which took place almost simultaneously with the ill-fated *putsch* in central Germany and which had been forced upon the Bolshevik regime by economic catastrophe and political upheaval, seemed to pay off in a most spectacular way. The abolition of the indiscriminate requisitioning of peasant produce in favor of a fixed tax, at first in kind and later in money; the opening of channels of trade through which the nontaxable part of peasant surplus could be freely sold; the denationalization of small-scale and medium-scale industry and trade; putting the bulk of the nationalized large-scale enterprises on the basis of "cost accounting" — all these policies represented a flagrant denial of the notions and beliefs about the nature of the "true" socialism which had been instilled in the minds of tens of thousands of party stalwarts during the period of Civil War — but they worked. The output of large-scale industry which had plummeted to 14 per cent of its prewar level by 1920 [1] rose to 46 per cent in 1924 and to 75 per cent in the following year. The marketable output of agriculture climbed by 64 per cent from 1922 to 1925.[2] Last but not least, the year 1924 saw the sum total of gross investment for the first time since 1917 exceed annual depreciation.[3]

Yet this development, while impressive and uninterrupted, was interlaced with tension which manifested itself in a variety of disturbances. The "scissors crisis" of 1923, which represented a contraction of rural markets for industrial goods, was followed slightly more than two years later by the "goods famine" — a Soviet term for repressed inflation. And along with these temporary disruptions, and obviously not unrelated to them, there were other more constant sources of anxiety. After having reached almost 40 per cent of its prewar volume by 1924, the marketable share of agricultural output showed only a very limited further increase.[4] In industry the recovery of prewar output levels was more rapid as well as more continuous. But here, too, there was a perceptible slackening after the huge forward leap of 1925; and it did not take a passion for progress to feel that the vicinity of the 1913 level which stamped Tsarist Russia as the most backward of the great powers of the world was not an ideal resting place.

These were the facts which set the stage and provided an impetus for the new turn in thinking. The successes of the NEP carried the Soviet economy beyond the range in which immediate survival was at stake, and enhanced the state's power to influence the course of events not merely by desisting from wrong-headed interference. But the jolts of imbalances and the steadily approaching ceilings for smooth increases indicated clearly that recovery was drawing to a close and that an enlargement of the capacity for growth was necessary. In Soviet parlance, the transition from "restoration" to "reconstruction" was impending. The perspective of protracted isolation within a hostile and much more powerful world, finally, made it imperative for the country to rely in this expansion upon its own resources, to a much greater extent than had been true of Tsarist Russia, or than had been hoped for in those heady years when the frontiers of the revolution seemed to lie on the Rhine.

It was at this point that the basic differences between the two ideological tournaments became visible. On the face of it, the Soviet controversy seemed an easier game because it could build on a framework laid several decades back, and because the fundamental disagreements of the old days were no longer present. All contestants were now as one in their refusal to romanticize Russian backwardness; to all of them industrialization was both the synonym of economic progress and an indispensable basis for a fully socialist society in the future. Actually, however, the theorists of the twenties faced a much more formidable task than their predecessors. The doctrine to which "fathers" as well as "sons" owned allegiance was a highly "dynamic" one. It was effective in throwing into focus a number of variables and structural relationships pertinent for the analysis of growth. It stressed the importance of discontinuous spurts in modern economic history; and it was most forceful in its description of the role of institutional changes and deliberate policies in the rise of industrial society. But when the writers of the eighties and nineties had used Marxist concepts and insights to interpret actually unfolding developmental processes and to rationalize their predilections for one course over another, they had been on firm ground; to use these devices for getting such a process started and for setting its pace was a very different matter. Beyond indicating a general direction in which to move and a few broad considerations to keep in mind, the "old books" could not provide any positive guidance here. They certainly did not contain operational advice for a situation in which a party, dedicated to the task of the socialist reconstruction of society, would come to power, not after industrialization had decisively reshaped the economic and social structure of the country in question, but at some point in the early and most difficult period of its transformation — and no adherents of Marxism had ever been more stage-conscious than the representatives of its prerevolutionary Russian brand.* In 1917–1921 the yawning

* It is true that Marx toward the close of his life seemed to sympathize with the Populist view according to which Russia could skip the stage of industrial capitalism in her development and base her socialist system on the peasant *obschchina* (village commune) which was to be transformed by an infusion of modern agricultural technology borrowed from the West. He elaborated on this point at some length in 1881 in reply to a query from Vera Zasulich, one of the founders of the Marxist movement in Russia. Marx did not show how this process of "borrowing" would actually work. Moreover, he qualified his position by stressing that the process of the dissolution of the *obschchina* was already well under way: only a revolution in the immediate future could, in his view, stop and reverse it.

gap between received doctrine and actual practice could be bridged, after a fashion, by the belief that revolutions in the industrialized West, coming on the heels of the October coup, would make the Soviet exception from the rule a more orthodox affair by helping to lift its shaky "basis" to the level of its advanced "superstructure." But these constructions went crashing to the ground in the years that followed.

In sum, the Soviet Marxists of the twenties were forced to recast their economics no less radically than their over-all political strategy. In the process of this revision they had to adapt Marxist theory to tasks for which it had not been designed, and to do this under conditions which had no place in its body of systematic analysis. This alone makes their debate a singularly exciting chapter in the history of economic doctrines; a chapter which is particularly worth exploring at a time when long-range growth has come again, after the lapse of nearly a century, to be one of the key concerns of economics, and when the presence of political

---

Actually, thirty-six years elapsed between this pronouncement and the revolution; in the meanwhile, the decomposition of the traditional agrarian setup continued apace, and so did the growth of modern industry. It is therefore not surprising that already in the mideighties the Russian Marxists wrote off the *obschchina* as a possible basis for socialist reconstruction and were emphatic in their insistence on the "historical inevitability of the Russian capitalism." It was hardly accidental, moreover, that Marx's reply to Vera Zasulich remained shelved for more than four decades. But by 1924 when this letter together with preliminary drafts was unearthed and published, it could not be very helpful. It was undoubtedly useful as evidence that Marx was not irrevocably committed to a rigid sequence of socioeconomic patterns and that he was aware of the "advantages of backwardness," a point which was stressed by Professor Alexander Gerschenkron. (See his paper, "The Problem of Economic Development in Russian Intellectual History of the Nineteenth Century," in Ernest J. Simmons, ed., *Continuity and Change in the Russian and Soviet Thought* [Cambridge, Massachusetts, 1955], pp. 35–36. For a detailed account of the Marx-Zasulich correspondence, see Solomon M. Schwarz, "Populism and Early Russian Marxism on Ways of Economic Development of Russia [The 1880's and 1890's]," *ibid.*, pp. 47–54.) But while the Soviet Marxists of the twenties had every reason to be grateful to the master for his readiness to skip stages, they must have felt that he had attempted to do it the wrong way.

elements in large economic decisions no longer causes apprehension. To be sure, the economist of today who follows these discussions cannot help being frequently dismayed by the unsystematic nature of the argument — important points are sometimes stated in an almost casual manner; analysis switches abruptly from one level to another or gets bogged down in terminological hairsplitting. Moreover, the leading debaters rarely take the trouble to buttress their diagnosis by statistical data. Yet, a Western student who, on account of technical inadequacies, disregards the ability of the Soviet theorists of the twenties to ask pertinent questions and to put forward suggestive solutions, refuses to see an imposing forest behind not-too-well-kept trees. Indeed, he is not very generous if he fails to acknowledge that both the problems raised and answers given anticipate to an astonishing degree the work done in the same field, at a much higher level of sophistication and within a different conceptual framework, by economists outside the Soviet orbit during the last two decades.

No doubt, the debate of the twenties lays a serious claim to our attention, also, on the grounds of its intrinsic merits alone. But it is idle to deny that this claim is immeasurably strengthened by the momentous nature of the actions which followed the words. The Soviet economic advance since 1928 has been one of the dominant facts of our time: there are few equally monumental truisms one can utter these days. The broad outlines of the pattern which emerged at the very beginning of the process have since then become familiar: a rate of investment set at a level which has few, if any, equals in the development of capitalist economies over a comparably long stretch of time; the overriding priority of producers' goods over consumers' goods in terms of the relative amount and quality of resources allotted to them; the change in terms of trade against agriculture, carried to unusual lengths for a country meeting the bulk of its food requirements from its own production. The results are history. According to the virtually unanimous view of Western students, the expansion of the Soviet industrial capacity has proceeded at a rate which is, by any meaningful standard of comparison, unprecedented. It is equally uncontroversial that this formidable drive, which has propelled the Soviet Union into the position of one of the two superpowers of the world, has entailed not only untold sacrifices in the welfare of the Soviet population but also grave risks for its rulers. Lags in low priority areas have resulted every now and then in major bottlenecks; convulsive shakeups and persistent all-pervading stresses and strains have cut into the efficiency of the huge investment efforts and have weakened the stability of the economy. Indeed, there is every indication that the whole system was more than once on the verge of explosion during its initial years.

What were the alternatives open to the Soviet economy at the end of the twenties? To what degree were Soviet leaders aware of their nature and potentialities? Did the actual course of events follow a design laid down well in advance or was it, to a significant extent, an improvised response to circumstances? These questions are central to the understanding and appraisal of the Soviet experience in accelerated industrialization. By studying the debate which preceded the First Five Year Plan, we can go a long way toward answering them. By exploring the many exchanges of views we can discover how the leading contestants saw the situation as it was unfolding between 1924 and 1928. By pursuing the ramifications of the argument, we can hope to determine to what extent their conflicting blueprints reflected different scales of preferences and underlying divergences in political orientation rather than disagreements about facts and analytical concepts. And then we may be able to find out how the interplay of the logic of facts and of the logic of basic attitudes made certain participants in the debate shift their positions — in case of the most strategically located discussant — in a very radical way. The results, it may be noted in advance, will not jibe with the official Stalinist account of the events — a point which should interest Western students, except perhaps for those who have chosen to assume, in a quasi-Hegelian spirit, that discarded alternatives are by definition inferior to the adopted ones. But this is certainly not the premise upon which the present study is based.

This leads us to another point. On the basis of all the foregoing one might conclude that the debate of the twenties is relevant only to a fairly remote, if crucially significant, stage in Soviet development. Indeed, until March 1953 it seemed so. The Western economist writing at that time did not have to subscribe to the "all that exists is rational" approach in order to feel that the deeply controversial issues of the twenties had been, for better or for worse, effectively brought under control, and that the system which had accomplished this feat would be likely, barring an international cataclysm, to remain intact for the foreseeable future. Now, seven years after Stalin's death, such a view is less firmly anchored in fact. Set patterns in the whole Soviet-controlled part of the globe have lost their stony immobility. Problems are reappearing; new "deviations" rear their heads; and amid stirrings of this dissent, old points of view, and, in the areas of highest tension, also the names of their protagonists, are brought forward by younger men who have been taught to despise or to ignore the work of the "enemies of the people." The ideas of the twenties are far from dead in our days.

The book is divided into two parts. Part I contains an account of the different points of view and of the changes which some of them underwent in the process of the debate. To keep the scope of this study within reasonable limits and to avoid unnecessary repetition, only those representatives of particular points of view who did not confine themselves to a few suggestive observations or to working out details of the argument, but who presented a more or less comprehensive set of ideas, are included. Part II restates the major issues of the debate in terms of Western analysis and subjects the positions of the individual participants to critical scrutiny. It begins with a discussion of views on the nature of the disequilibrating forces which were at work in the Soviet economy; it deals next with the possibilities of reducing tension by the appropriate allocation of investment among sectors and projects with varying capital requirements and by deriving maximum advantage from foreign trade; and it concludes with a reappraisal of these possibilities in the light of long-term considerations. The problems involved are much too formidable to be discussed exhaustively within the compass of the present study, and this writer's comments are not to be construed as an attempt at such discussion. They intend to do no more than to indicate his position on the issues in question. The last chapter attempts to explain why the compromise solution after having been adopted by the party leadership and, more particularly, by Stalin, was nevertheless discarded in the end. The writer was confronted by a choice between letting this question go unanswered or making a deep foray into the territory of the political scientists; in spite of all its attendant hazards, he chose the latter. The analysis concludes with a few observations about the relevance of the controversy for the developments of the post-Stalin era.

PART ONE

The Debate

I

The "Lenin Revolution" and
Its Interpreter

"THE switch of trains we made in the spring of 1921 . . . was dictated by circumstances which were so overpowering and convincing that there were no debates and no differences of opinions among us." [1] This appraisal made twenty months after the event was undoubtedly correct; yet, it contained more than a grain of disarming modesty on the part of its author. The momentous decision to abandon War Communism did not, and could not, cause any significant discord; in the face of the economic debacle and the rising tide of popular unrest there was no other choice. It would therefore seem obvious to accept and to explain the new course as a plain and simple retreat carried out in order to stave off immediate collapse; indeed, this was the prevailing attitude. It took quite exceptional political and intellectual resilience to go beyond this explanation and to perceive in a staggering setback potentialities for advance toward the same ultimate goal along a route more roundabout than the old but also safer. And it was Lenin who again displayed his ability not only to lead his party through a most drastic change in its policy but also to reformulate at shortest notice its whole strategy, and to throw overboard without hesitation cherished concepts, scales of priorities, and habits of thought. True, the transition to the NEP represented less of a shift for its author than for most of his collaborators: Lenin had every right to point out that he had advocated a similar setting already in early 1918. Yet subsequently he had veered away from this position much further than could be explained solely by the pressure of the exigencies of the Civil War — a fact he was candid enough to acknowledge on a later occasion when he spoke of the "wave of enthusiasm" which had gripped the Bolsheviks and had made them "reckon on being able to organize the state production and state distribution of products on communist lines in a small-peasant country directly on orders of proletarian state." "Experience," he went on, "has proved that we were wrong." [2] Moreover, while the specific proposals resembled the blueprint discarded three years ago, the insights into the mode of operation of the system and into its future prospects were strikingly new.

The crucial task, Lenin stressed in his pamphlet, *The Tax in Kind,* was "to improve the conditions of the peasantry and to increase their productive forces."

Why the peasantry and not the workers?
Because in order to improve the conditions of the workers, grain and fuel are required. This is the biggest "hitch" at the present time, from the point of view of the national economy as a whole. And it is impossible to increase the production and collection of grain and the collection and delivery of fuel except by improving the conditions of the peasantry, by raising their productive forces. We must start with the peasantry. Those who fail to understand this, those who are inclined to regard this putting the peasantry in the forefront as a "renunciation" or something similar to the renunciation of the dictatorship of the proletariat, simply do not stop to think, and yield to the power of words.

The essence of [the] peculiar War Communism was that we actually took from the peasant all the surplus grain — and sometimes even not only surplus grain but part of the grain the peasant required for food — to meet the requirements of the army and to sustain the workers. Most of it we took on loan, for paper money. . . . We were forced to resort to War Communism by war and ruin. It was not, nor could it be, a policy that corresponded to the economic tasks of the proletariat. . . . The correct policy of the proletariat which is exercising its dictatorship in a small-peasant country is to obtain grain in exchange for the manufactured goods the peasant requires. . . .

After explaining that the newly reproduced "tax in kind" represented the first step in this direction ("We shall take the minimum of grain we require for the army and the workers in the form of a tax and will obtain the rest in exchange for manufactured goods"), Lenin continued:

Our poverty and ruin are so great that we cannot *at one stroke* restore large-scale, factory, state socialist production. This requires that we accumulate large stocks of grain and fuel in the big industrial centers, replace the worn-out machines with new ones, and so on. Experience has convinced us that this cannot be done at one stroke. . . .

This sturdy piece of orthodox scarcity economics was followed by a set of conclusions which seemed as startling in its economic content as in its sociopolitical implications. Lenin recommended a determined effort toward attracting private investment from the West by leasing out large sections of the manufacturing and extractive industries. Imports of capital obtained at the price of these "concessions" would "secure an increased quantity of goods immediately, or within a very short period" and, at the same time, "strengthen large-scale production as against small production, advanced production as against backward production, machine [operated] production as against hand-labor production." But this dearly bought inflow of resources from the outside could not relieve the Soviet leadership of the necessity to lower their sights:

It is necessary, to a certain extent, to help to restore *small* industry which does not need machines, does not need either state reserves or large stocks of raw material, fuel, and food and which can immediately render some assistance to peasant farming and increase its productive forces.

What will be the effect of this? The effect will be the revival of the petty bourgeoisie and of capitalism on the basis of a certain amount of free trade (if only local). This is beyond doubt. It would be ridiculous to shut our eyes to it. . . .

[Should we] try to prohibit entirely, to put the lock on, all development of private, nonstate exchange, i.e., trade, i.e., capitalism which is inevitable and amidst millions of small producers? But such a policy would be foolish and suicidal for a party that tried to apply it. . . .

Lenin was even more emphatic in summing up and in spelling out the particulars:

There is obviously a delay in the restoration of large-scale production, and the locking up of exchange between industry and agriculture has become intolerable. Consequently, we must concentrate all efforts on what is more accessible — the restoration of small industry. . . . *We must do everything possible to develop trade at all costs*, without being afraid of capitalism, because the limits we have put to it . . . are sufficiently narrow, sufficiently moderate. This is the fundamental idea of the tax in kind, this is its economic significance.

. . . Local or imported salt; kerosene from the center; the handicraft wood-working industry; handicrafts using local raw materials, and producing certain, not very important perhaps, but nevertheless necessary and useful articles for the peasants; "white coal" (the utilization of small local water-power resources for electrification), and so on and so forth — all this must be set going in order to stimulate exchange between industry and agriculture at all costs. Those who achieve the best results in this sphere, even by means of private capitalism, even without cooperatives, without directly transforming this capitalism into state capitalism, will do more for the cause of all-Russian Socialist construction than those who will "ponder over" the purity of Communism, draw up regulations, rules, and instructions for state capitalism and the cooperatives, but do nothing practical to stimulate trade.[3]

Lenin never retreated from this position. No doubt, as the immediate emergency receded, the emphasis on long-term issues and prospects in his enunciations kept increasing; and here, too, new departures became discernible. He qualified more drastically than ever before a fundamental tenet of prerevolutionary Russian Marxism, which he himself had once fully shared, when he declared, in a polemical gloss on Sukhanov's *Notes on Revolution,* that in certain situations the proletarian seizure of power could precede and make possible the achievement of the preconditions for a full-fledged socialism rather than having to wait until they had been established in the process of capitalist development. It was in this context that the fateful notion of "catching-up" was brought in:

If a definite level of culture is required for the building of socialism (although nobody can say just what this definite "level of culture" is, for it differs in every West European country), why cannot we begin by first achieving the prerequisites for that definite level of culture in a revolutionary way, and *then,* with the aid of the workers' and peasants' government and the Soviet system, proceed to catch up with other nations? . . . Why could we not first create such preconditions of civilization in our country as the expulsion of the landlords and the Russian capitalists, and then start moving toward socialism? [4]

In his last article this idea broadened into vision:

If we shall see to it that the working class retains the leadership of the peasantry, we shall be able, by exercising the greatest possible parsimony in the economy of our state, to use everything we save to develop our large-scale machine [operated] industry, to develop electrification, the hydraulic extraction of peat, to finish the construction of Volkhovstroi, etc. In this, and in this alone lies our hope. . . .[5]

Yet no doubts were left as to the anticipated tempo of the movement toward this goal. In the same article which bore the characteristic caption: "Better Fewer But Better" (*Luch-she men'she, da luchshe*), Lenin called for "a salutary scepticism toward the rapid-fire speed in advancing" when he warned against pushing the growth of state apparatus in utter disregard of the shortage of skilled and responsible civil servants. The same injunction applied, as he made clear time and time again, in the field of economic policy as well:

We must and we can achieve an increase in productive forces, if need be on the level of small-scale peasant economy and for the time being on the basis of the small-scale industry if the restoration of the large scale is so difficult. . . . Here we cannot achieve our aims as rapidly as we could do it in the political and military sphere. Here we cannot move by leaps and bounds, and the time table is different — it is measured by decades. Such is the time period during which we will have to seek successes in the economic war and in conditions not of assistance but of hostility on the part of our neighbors.[6]

Our aim . . . is to prove to the peasant by deeds that we are beginning with what is intelligible, familiar and immediately accessible to him in spite of his poverty, and not with something remote and fantastic from the peasant's point of view; we must prove that we can help him. . . . Either we prove that, or he will send us to the devil. That is absolutely inevitable. . . .

Link up with the peasant masses, with the rank-and-file toiling peasants, and begin to move forward immeasurably, infinitely more slowly than we expected but in such a way that the entire mass will actually move forward with us. If we do that we shall in time get an acceleration of this movement such as we cannot dream of now.[7]

The impact of the "Lenin Revolution" was not immediately evident; the grim task of digging out of the wreckage left little room for choice and was not propitious for the discussion of fundamentals. Yet the flareup of controversy which came after the stage of struggle for bare survival was over revealed with striking clarity how widely and how deeply Lenin's new ideas had taken hold. These were the ideas which Nikolai I. Bukharin chose as a point of departure when he formulated his position on crucial issues of economic policy three and one-half years later. The profound change in the prevalent mood was personalized, as it were, thereby. Bukharin had belonged after October 1917 to the group which had opposed the peace of Brest-Litovsk and which had continued ever since as the extremist faction of the Bolshevik party, pressing most relentlessly for the extension of nationalization and for direct controls all over the economy. His *Ekonomika perekhodnogo perioda* (Economy of the Transition Period) was the theoretical manifesto of War Communism. He was undoubtedly the best-educated economist not only of his group, but of the whole party as well, with a truly astounding facility for the rationalization, in terms of theory, of any political viewpoints he happened to embrace, and for pushing them toward the furthest logical consequences. And if the *Ekonomika* made some of Bukharin's friends shudder at the extremism of its assumptions and conclusions, so did his swing to the opposite direction.

Bukharin started out by restating in a generalized form Lenin's characterization of War Communism. The essence of the economic policy of that period, he contended, lay in its emphasis upon the redistribution of the given real income rather than upon securing its continuous reproduction on an expanded scale. In order to achieve the latter task, it is not enough to have at hand the physical resources; the disparate factors of production can be combined in productive processes only when their owners have a palpable personal incentive to do so. In the period of War Communism such an incentive existed neither for the peasants who were forcibly deprived of their surplus without getting anything in return, nor for the workers whose remuneration bore no relationship to their productive contribution. With regard to that period, Bukharin felt, Mises' strictures against economic mismanagement under socialism were largely justified. There was, however, no reason for the Soviet economic policy to continue along the same lines after the emergency of the Civil War was over. No obstacles and no ideological inhibitions should now be permitted to stand in the way of "unlocking the trade" which would help to bring the production factors together. Instead of killing the hens that laid the golden eggs, one had to let them grow:

By using the economic initiative of peasants, small producers, and even bourgeois, by tolerating subsequently private accumulation, we are putting them objectively to the service of the socialist state industry and of the economy as a whole: this is what the meaning of the NEP consists in. By developing trade we have restored the operation of the personal incentive of the small-scale producers, we have stimulated the expansion of output, we have put to the service of socialism the individualist strata of the workers, motivated not by communist ideas but by their private interests, through introduction of the old type of wage payments (piece work, etc.). . . .

Bukharin did not hesitate to admit that such a policy would imply a basic revision of the accepted views on socialist planning:

According to our former concepts, we considered it possible to achieve the planned economy almost at once. Our present concepts are different. We occupy the commanding heights, we establish the key positions firmly; and then our state economy by different ways, sometimes even by competition with the remnants of private capital, keeps increasing its strength and gradually absorbs the backward economic units — a process which occurs in the main through the market.[8]

◘

On closer scrutiny, it is quite clear that the notion of "market" meant to Bukharin two different things. Its function as a stimulant for personal incentive was in his analysis inseparable from its "macroeconomic" performance as the absorber of aggregate output. He systematized his views on the second aspect of the problem by an excursion into the "theory of realization," outlined in the second volume of Marx's *Capital* and discussed at great length in Marxian literature. Bukharin rejected Rosa Luxemburg's thesis that in a market economy, consisting solely of capitalists and workers, the reinvestment of profits and the resulting expansion would inevitably lead to crisis because there would be no increase in demand to match the increase in supply. The wages of new workers, he reasoned, could buy the increment in mass-consumption goods, and the consumed part of the increased profits would provide the outlet for the addition to the output of luxuries while the accumulated part would help to absorb the enlarged volume of investment goods. (The possibility that planned savings-out-of-profits could exceed investment had no place in his scheme of things nor, for that matter, in any other version of Marxian macroeconomic analysis.) Yet while the lag in final demand behind the increase in total output was, in his view, not a built-in permanent feature of the capitalist economy, it would be well-nigh inevitable as a sporadic occurrence owing to the "anarchic structure" of capitalism. And given the fact that "the lines which are producing means of production represent *preparatory stages of the production of means of consumption* whatever their size may be," [9] the failure of consumers' demand to keep in step with productive capacity could not but cause a contraction in both major subdivisions of the economy. Consequently, while Bukharin strongly disagreed with Rosa Luxemburg, he was even more vehement in attacking Tugan Baranovski's theory according to which the output of investment goods could (within the limits set by the nonaugmentable natural resources) keep increasing infinitely with consumption lagging behind or even declining.

These findings, he felt, were directly relevant to the Soviet situation. Under Russian conditions the proportionality between production and consumption hinged primarily on the relationship between the size of the urban industry and the level of the effective demand of the peasant population. "The relative narrowness of the internal market brought Tsarism down";[10] and the "scissors crisis" of 1923 provided a dramatic reminder that the Soviet system was exposed to dangers of the same type if "applied Tuganism" should prevail. But this very crisis which was the most serious disturbance since the inception of the NEP showed at the same time the proper way of dealing with the difficulties involved:

It sufficed to press the price down and it became clear that (1) industry started to develop much faster and the demand began to outstrip the supply; (2) industrial profits did not disappear at all; (3) the tempo of accumulation increased; (4) agriculture began to grow faster at the same time; (5) economic growth all along the line followed.[11]

The above lines anticipated a question which was bound to arise in connection with the proposed line of action and which was to play a most important role in the Soviet economic discussion. The general lowering of industrial prices was for Bukharin not merely an inevitable adjustment to the limited demand, but also a starting point for a great upward surge. Here again a happy coincidence between "microeconomic" and "macroeconomic" considerations existed, with the causal relationship operating this time from the first to the second — the behavior which would be correct from the viewpoint of a single firm in the competitive market was certain to result in an advance of the economy as a whole. The price reduction would, indeed, cut the profit per unit of output. But it would at the same time increase the volume of sales (as well as shorten the period during which the stocks of unsold goods were piling up and causing additional costs of storage).* The total volume of profits would, consequently, increase.

No less important would be, in the long run, another effect of the same policy. The elimination of easy monopolistic gains by a slash in prices would shake plant managers out of their complacency and impel them to strive actively for improvement in methods of production. The ghost of "parasitic decay" would thus be effectively laid and the absorption capacity of the market would grow as unit costs declined. Also, in the sphere of foreign economic relations the removal (or at least relaxation) of monopolistic restrictions would stimulate expansion of domestic output and growth of trade — a point which Bukharin made in his critique of the foreign trade monopoly in the fall of 1922 and to which he stuck also in later years. The influx of cheap foreign goods, he argued, would bring about an increase in the productivity of the domestic economy by giving a boost to peasants' production for market and by stimulating expansion in industries whose products were complementary to imported goods. The over-all increase in the demand for industrial products resulting from such development would be practically cer-

* See "Novoe otkrovenie o sovetskoi ekonomike ili kak mozhno pogubit' raboche-krest'yanski blok," B (December 10, 1924), p. 52. The argument about excessive stocks is not convincing. Clearly, such an excess was not due to the low volume of sales *per se* but to the fall of this volume below the planned level as a result of an unexpectedly low demand. But while it was certainly quite appropriate for the administrators of Soviet industry to respond to such a predicament by lowering prices and thus getting rid of unsaleable goods, the implications for the next step were less clearcut. A reduction in output to the volume which could still be sold at the planned high price under the prevailing demand conditions would, after a relatively short time-lag, bring about a downward adjustment in stock just as effectively as the alternative method of maintaining a larger scale of output in conjunction with the lower prices. From the viewpoint of overstocking, consequently, there was no reason to prefer one procedure to the other. The situation was different, of course, with regard to the durable equipment which had been installed in anticipation of a higher output level and could be adjusted downward much slower than the stock of "goods in process"; but this is not what Bukharin had in mind.

tain to swamp whatever depressing effects the imports in question might have on the domestic output of similar kind.

What does the imported tractor do? It *immediately* increases the agricultural output. This implies an increase in the absorption capacity of the internal market, increased demand for products of industry (both consumers goods and investment goods), increase in agricultural exports; the tractors, in turn are creating demand for oil, etc., etc. But all this creates, eventually, an additional demand for tractors as well (general growth of agriculture, export, etc.). It is foolish to think of demand or even of the rate of accumulation as of something fixed. The basis for the domestic tractor output is not destroyed, and it will be necessary to throw in this whole output when the limits of production are extended.[12]

It may seem paradoxical, on the face of it, that while Bukharin took such a "liberal" attitude in the question of foreign trade, he paid no attention to the problem of capital imports; in fact, he took obvious satisfaction in pinning the label of "half-Menshevism" on his adversaries who emphasized the importance of foreign investment. In this respect, he sharply differed from Lenin who was outspokenly in favor of the policy of "concessions." True, the economic situation in 1924 was much less desperate than three years earlier and this may have permitted rejection of some obviously distasteful recipes, but there is no evidence that Lenin considered foreign investment merely a drastic emergency measure. The main cause of disagreement seemed to lie elsewhere. To Bukharin the policy of "developing trade at all costs" was not merely a necessary but also a sufficient condition for a complete restoration of the large-scale industry. The originator of this strategy was less optimistic, and with good reasons, as will be shown later.

□

The reduction of industrial prices accompanied by a general shake-up of industry was not the only way in which the limits of the market could be extended. The problem was to be tackled also from the opposite end. The effective demand of the peasants for the output of industry, Bukharin argued, will increase only if they are able to raise the level of their income by enlarging and improving their production facilities through steady investment. This growth of peasant economy, however, cannot get underway as long as individuals who have the means and the will to such expansion are hemmed in by laws prohibiting the use of hired labor and are subject to incessant discriminations and penalties:

The well-to-do stratum of the peasantry and the middle peasant who wants to become well-to-do *are afraid to accumulate* nowadays. A situation is created in which the peasant is afraid to cover his house with an iron roof because he is afraid to be branded a "kulak"; if he buys a machine he does it in such a way as to hide it from the communists. The higher technology becomes conspiratve. . . . The well-to-do peasant is dissatisfied because we do not let him accumulate and hire farm hands; on the other hand, the poor peasants who suffer from overpopulation are grumbling because they are not permitted to hire themselves.[13]

All these institutional and psychological left-overs of the War Communist period which were so obviously incongruous with the spirit of the NEP had to be eradicated. The "forced normalization" of the regime was imperative: "The peasant must face Soviet order, Soviet law, and not Soviet arbitrariness, moderated by a 'bureau of complaints' whose location is unknown."[14] The restrictions on hire of labor had to be lifted, or at least relaxed.

To these proposals, which were essentially of a negative nature, Bukharin added a positive recommendation. The all-out promotion of peasant cooperation was, in his view, the most important constructive contribution which could be made in the field of agricultural economy by the Soviet regime. The cooperative organization should be primarily confined, at first, to the "sphere of circulation" like the marketing of agricultural products, the purchase of industrial goods, and the supply of credit; the identity of the peasants as independent small-scale producers would in the vast majority of cases be retained for a considerable period of time. Here, once more, the motive force of individual interest would powerfully promote social ends. The peasants would have very palpable incentives for joining cooperatives which would enable them to improve the terms of trade and gain access to the sources of cheap credit, thus lessening their dependence from village usurers.

It is correct that we must propagandize in all possible ways the merger into collective farms. It is wrong, however, when it is maintained that this is the *main* road along which the bulk of the peasantry will advance toward socialism. How should we then attract the peasantry to our socialist system? Only by making it economically attractive to the peasants. The cooperative should appeal to the peasant by giving him immediate benefits. If it is a credit cooperative, he will get cheap credit, if it is a marketing cooperative, he will sell his product on better terms. If he wants to buy something, he will get better quality and cheaper goods.[15]

A stimulus was to be imparted to the improvement in the peasant economy which would, in turn, accelerate the advance of industry. As a result of this development through mutual interaction, one branch of the agricultural economy after the other would eventually outgrow the limits of individual peasant holdings and remodel itself along the lines of large-scale production and of collective ownership.

It was in this context that Bukharin disinterred Guizot's famous "enrichissez-vous" which was later to haunt him for years: "We have to tell the whole peasantry, all its strata: get rich, accumulate, develop your economy." * He

* "O novoi ekonomicheskoi politike i nashikh zadachakh," part II, *B* (June 1, 1925), p. 5. This formula produced quite a stir and Bukharin had to retract it three times shortly afterwards; he did not, however, renounce the underlying idea. See VKP, *XIV s'ezd* (Moscow-Leningrad, 1926), p. 150.

made no attempt to deny that the development envisaged by him might enhance the economic power of the group which was considered the strongest remnant of capitalism in Soviet society and the potential basis for its restoration. But the proper way of meeting these grave problems consisted, in his view, neither in curbing the rise of the rich peasantry by restrictions and prohibitions nor in setting one's face toward the "second revolution" which would put an end to the new upper stratum in the villages just as the revolution of 1917 had done with regard to the old. The Soviet state could take recourse to methods which would involve no such shocks and disturbances — the economically rational could be reconciled with the socially desirable. The growth of cooperation would raise the economic level of the peasantry as a whole and thus sap the foundations of the kulak's power. True, the kulaks also could avail themselves of this superior technique of organization either by setting up cooperatives of their own or by infiltrating those created by others. But the gains secured by poor and medium peasants who had been previously to a varying extent dependent on the village rich, would be much greater, particularly since they would have on their side the all-out support of the state. The sharply progressive taxation would narrow the income differentials still further. Moreover, part of the disposable income of the kulaks would be saved and drawn into the nexus of the socialized sector of the economy and contribute to its expansion through the channels of a nationalized credit system.* The end result of this gradual levelling and increasing dependence on state-controlled "commanding heights" would be a euthanasia of the kulak after he had very much against his will rendered a yeoman

* "If we are walking around naked, the kulak will conquer us economically, and if he is a depositor in our banks, he won't conquer us. We are helping him, but he is helping us, too . . . ," B (April 30, 1925), p. 14.

service to the socialist economy; a classical piece of Hegelian *List der Vernunft*.

Such was, in essence, Bukharin's position around the middle of the twenties. Its political underpinnings were not difficult to discover; in fact, Bukharin had no compunctions about making them explicit. He was battling against the Trotskyite notion that the individualistic peasantry, after helping the urban proletariat to seize power and to maintain it against the forces of monarchy and landlordism, must inevitably turn against its ally when the latter started to push on toward the socialist reorganization of society. The cooperation of industrial workers with the main body of peasantry was no less indispensable in the business of maintaining and strengthening the socialist foundations than in the process of gaining power and winning the civil war; this was to him the major lesson of the events of 1921 as well as of the "scissors crisis" of 1923. The task consisted in proving that such a "bloc" was not merely necessary but also feasible. Hopes for the world revolution did not, in Bukharin's view, point to any quick way around the problem. Not only the prospects of such a revolution appeared more remote in the midtwenties than they had ever been since the Bolshevik victory, but, also, its ultimate triumph would at first merely reproduce the Russian configuration of forces on a worldwide scale, with the proletarians of the West heavily outnumbered by the peasant masses of the underdeveloped East.[16]

It was this basic attitude which caused Bukharin to go all-out in search of a policy which would permit the achievements of a workable compromise between the two partners of the "bloc" and to maintain it along all the twists and turns of the road. In so doing, he was often less than discriminating in his choice of arguments and somewhat cavalier in his ways of presenting them. His violent assault against Tugan Baranovski was a case in point. Bukharin was on the wrong track when he kept insisting that today's investment cannot mature into anything else but the increased consumption of the future. He did not notice that the crucial issue at stake was not the technological possibility of "building mills that should make more mills forever" (to borrow J. B. Clark's famous phrase), but the economic rationale of the staggering rate of increase in capital stock which such a policy would entail. In other words, he lacked the notion of declining investment opportunity just as much as his opponents did. It was therefore not surprising that he did not stop to inquire to what extent planned and unplanned economies differ in this particular respect. The few remarks to the effect that the share of producers goods in the total output of the economy would grow faster under socialism than under capitalism as a result of quicker pace of the technological progress,[17] were no substitute for such an inquiry; and the specific criticisms by which he attempted to back the attack were not helpful. He was off the mark, for example, when he dramatically asked, "what will happen" to the increase in the output of goods coming as a result of the introduction of new machinery? [18] If the goods in question were capital goods, Tugan Baranovski's economy would always have a ready outlet for them; and should they be consumers goods as Bukharin apparently assumed, the increase in the output per man could be entirely compatible with constancy or even with decline in the total output of the industry affected by the innovation, and with the continual shift of resources toward a self-expanding capital-goods sector. Here, once again, the thing to do was to probe into the basic assumption that this sector could always be relied upon to expand whenever consumption would decline — but this was precisely what neither Bukharin nor other Marxist critics of Tugan Baranovski ever attempted. His remark that the expansion of output of investment goods would entail an increase in the demand for consumers goods on the part of newly employed workers suffered from a similar failure to pay attention to the specific assumptions of the criticized theory. In the Tuganist scheme of things the total volume of employment would not increase but remain constant or, more likely, decline over time as a result of the massive and uncompensated technological displacement of labor. But even if this assumption were abandoned, the "demand for consumers goods" would result in a wage-price spiral rather than in an increase in consumption as long as the self-propelled investment continued to expand.

Besides, and more important, the way in which the results of the analysis were applied to the problems on hand was clearly misguided. Even if Bukharin had been everlastingly right on all the counts of his indictment, he would have proved that a policy of pushing investment ahead of consumption was bound to cause an excess of supply over demand, but not before the new plant had been completed and put into operation. It would be certainly odd to consider this a good explanation for a crisis of glut in an economy which was just about to resume the construction of its plant. Nor was it immediately evident why the peasant demand should be considered particularly crucial and why a demand coming from other sources could not compensate its decline. Such a notion makes sense only from the underconsumptionist viewpoint which, as we saw a while ago, was resolutely condemned. In fact, Bukharin conceded this in so many words. He tried to protect himself by switching to a less fundamentalist level and by stressing the difficulties of readjustment for an economy which had once been geared in a definite direction.

The Populists maintained that accumulation is impossible in general without the third persons [neither workers nor capitalists]. This thesis is wrong. But it should not be confused with the other question; namely, if a system of economic relationships is given in which industry has already worked for the peasant market, and in which it cannot exist *without* the connection with this market, then the state of industrial business, tempo of accumulation, etc., cannot be independent from the growth of the productive forces of agriculture.[19]

But although these observations contained an element of truth, it was not strong enough to sustain the argument.

Yet all this confusion was not, in itself, fatal to the case Bukharin wanted to make. When he argued that the key problem of the Soviet economy of the midtwenties revolved around the relations between state industry and peasant agriculture, and that the development of the first was dependent on the rise of the second, he was undoubtedly right. In order to prove it, he did not have to raise the specter of "applied Tuganism" or to call in technological rigidities because the elements of less forced explanation were within his grasp. He put his finger on the crucial spot when he spoke of "setting into movement the factors of production which are lying idle like a dead weight" and of mobilizing "the hidden reserves of energy," [20] as well as of "more intensive utilization of the unit of capital." [21] This was, indeed, the basic fact from which all the rest followed. Soviet large-scale industry in the early years of the NEP could have increased its output without any prior expansion of its plant because large reserves of unused capacity were available. But such an increase could not come about without stepping up the volume as well as the efficiency of the labor force employed in operating this plant, and neither of these was possible without larger food supplies. Moreover, important parts of the processing industries could not be put into operation without raw material of agricultural origin; and as channels of foreign trade were gradually reopening, exports of grain could again perform their traditional role of buying foreign capital goods for the Russian industry.

In view of all this, to put the chief emphasis on the im-

portance of peasant demand, as Bukharin did, seemed odd.
Yet while he did not get hold of the right end of the stick,
he did get hold of the stick — and this was at that time of
the day more than satisfactory for all practical intents and
purposes. The Soviet government could, theoretically speaking, counter the collapse of peasant demand by compensatory
boosts to spending in the urban sector although the differences in the consumption pattern would require some
reorientation in industrial production — an operation which
would be not easy to carry out in view of the dilapidated
condition of the Soviet capital-goods industry at that time.
(We will hear much more about the last-mentioned point
later.) But there was no comparable possibility of softening
the blow which the limited flow of marketable agricultural
produce would deal to the urban sector. In other words,
while the peasant demand was more expendable than the
peasant supply, the latter could not be had, except in utterly
inadequate amounts, unless the first had been given proper
attention. The experience of War Communism established
this beyond the possibility of doubt. By the same token,
a policy of catering to peasant demand would start a chain
reaction in the opposite direction. By offering the peasants
better terms of trade than a consistently "monopolistic" price
policy would have permitted, the urban industry would
benefit in the long run; it would have at its disposal larger
amounts of agricultural products. This, in turn, would make
it possible to step up the utilization of the idle industrial
capacity still further, with all the cost economies which such
a possibility would entail, and thereby start new cycles of
over-all increase. Bukharin must have had such a development in mind when he declared that "the proletariat has
in its hands, given a rising curve of productive forces, the
law of large-scale production." [22] "When the upswing starts,"
he insisted, "the dominant role of the town becomes im-
pregnable, and because we have already entered this stage,

there is every reason to assume that by increasing in strength at a growing rate we will achieve a very quick tempo of growth." [23] Similarly, it was perfectly logical for him to argue that imposition of curbs on "easy" monopolistic profits would put the managers of Soviet enterprises under strong pressure to minimize their costs by introducing organizational and technological improvements. Some of them (he might have added) would not require any additional investment on a substantial scale in view of the slack which is bound to be present in the industrial system of a backward country, particularly after a long spell of civil war and inflation. And there could be no doubt that the "forced normalization" in the villages and the renewal of uncertainty which had been weakening the peasants' incentive to apply superior methods of production, would operate in the same direction.

In sum, Bukharin came very close to establishing a strong case on grounds which were in part quite shaky and in part perfectly tenable, although not fully stated. His optimistic horoscopes certainly were not pulled entirely out of a hat. Yet his underlying assumptions never represented the whole story; and, what was much more serious, they were already on their way out when Bukharin was confidently extrapolating them into the future. The penchant for enthusiastic and rash generalization made him overplay his hand as he had done once before. Four years earlier he had offered a most polished and theoretically sophisticated defense of War Communism, only to see the object of his adulation discarded within a couple of months. Now he hailed the "normalcy" of the NEP as the surest route to recovery and to further growth without noticing the approach of a new and no less fateful turning of the road. It was others who rose to the challenge.

II

The Challenge from the Right
and the Left

ONE of the first and most determined attempts to face
the new situation was made toward the end of 1925. Its
originators were Lev M. Shanin, a ranking member of the
staff of the People's Commissariat of Finance, and Grigori Ya.
Sokol'nikov, a Bolshevik leader of old standing and former
head of the same Commissariat. The two men did not speak
on behalf of any distinctive group. In fact, Sokol'nikov took
pains to disclaim the similarity between his position and
that of his old colleague in the speech at the Fourteenth
Party Congress (December 1925) in which he came out in
support of the leftist "Leningrad opposition," while Shanin,
in an article which appeared shortly afterward, copiously
quoted Stalin and Rykov in order to make his views more
palatable. Yet their attitudes on economic problems were
practically identical. They represented, no doubt, the furthest point in the reconsideration of fundamentals which
the NEP had brought about within the Communist ranks.
They also reflected the clear realization that the heyday of
the recovery was over:

There was a time when our enterprises were operating with a
very light load. In that period it sufficed to make minor repairs,
minor investment into fixed capital in order to obtain a quick
increase in the load. . . . And since each increase in load caused
a decline in unit costs of output, the investment of new circulat-

ing capital caused not merely an immediate increase in output, but also its considerable cheapening.

Now it is different. The enterprises are loaded to a sufficiently full extent. . . . We are now activizing . . . the enterprises which are technologically most backward, which require extensive repair work and which cannot after all these outlays give a cheaper output than enterprises of first and second category. Now each expenditure of new capital is to a larger extent an investment in fixed capital than before. . . .[1]

Nor was this all; some sectors of industry were more affected by this change than others:

As long as the plant was there, we needed, in the heavy as well as in the light industry, only circulating funds in order to put our enterprises into operation, and on the whole, the production effects were achieved equally fast in both of them. . . . But now when we switch from the restoration process to the construction of new plants or to the reconditioning of old plants . . . each new investment in heavy industry calls for much larger expenditures than an investment in light industry while the production effects will be coming forward later in the first case. . . .[2]

The diagnosis was sobering, and so was the prescription for setting the size and the direction of the total investment. "The main criterion determining the volume of the permissible expansion of the fixed capital and setting the maximum limit for investment, is the availability of commodity reserves provided by the economic activity of the preceding period or imported on the basis of loan,"[3] and, given the precarious level of these reserves in the Soviet economy around the end of 1925, the "maximum limit" had to be kept correspondingly low. For the same reasons, the Soviet economy could not afford to give priority to those types of investment which would tie up the resources diverted from current consumption for a long time before starting to deliver the goods and which would swell the volume of spending in the meanwhile. In absence of the accumulated stocks of finished goods which could be thrown upon the market in order to bridge the gap, such a policy could not but result in a goods famine, that is, repressed inflation, which was in fact harrowing the Soviet economy in the winter of 1925–26. The main emphasis had therefore to be put on investment in agriculture which "requires an incomparably smaller outlay of capital per unit of output" and which "will throw the goods upon the market much faster than industry." [4] Within the nonagricultural field, "light" industries absorbing relatively little capital and based largely on agricultural raw material were to be promoted more than capital-intensive "heavy" industries. The only major exception was to be made for the highly capital-absorbing transportation system, whose development was a key to "increase of turnover" on the basis of existing productive capacity and whose services would not, unlike the products of industry, be imported from abroad.

◻

The immediate advantage of such a pattern of priorities would be, on the face of it, to smooth the difficult transition from "restoration" to "reconstruction." But Shanin and Sokol'nikov aimed higher than that — to them this arrangement represented also the optimal pattern of long-range economic development. In the initial stage, Shanin admitted, the tempo of industrial growth would indeed be slower than if the reversed priority order had been chosen. But in the long run the process of industrialization would be accelerated, and not delayed, by putting agriculture first. The first reason for this seemingly paradoxical theorem followed closely from the foregoing argument. A ruble invested in "less capitalistic" agriculture would yield a greater volume of output than in the "more capitalistic" industry, and would result in a higher rate of capital formation.

⅄ The organic structure of capital in agriculture is much lower [than in industry]. . . . A unit of capital in agriculture sets into motion eight times as much labor as in industry. Given the same rate of exploitation of labor, a unit of capital gives a much larger accumulation in industry than in agriculture. Besides, the level of consumption is low; and this reinforces the accumulation effect.[5]

Ⅺ Consequently, if the whole investable surplus of the peasant economy had been plowed back into agriculture, permitted to grow at a high rate for several years, and only afterwards invested into industry, the total effect achieved within the whole period would have been much greater if this surplus had been channeled into industry right from the start.

While the average rate of accumulation in industry can be estimated at 6 per cent, the rate of accumulation in agriculture should be estimated at 15 per cent. . . . If 100 units of resources were shifted this year from agriculture into industry, they would yield in the second year 106, in the third year 112.3, in the fourth year 119.1 additional units. But if these original 100 units had been permitted to remain in agriculture, they would have yielded 115.0 additional units in the second year, 132.2 in the third year, and 152.0 in the fourth year. . . . If the shift to resources [from agriculture to industry] had taken place not in the first year, but at the beginning of the fifth, the resources of industry, given the input of the same 100 additional units, would increase by 152.0, instead of by 119.2.[6]

This shift, moreover, would have been still more advantageous if undertaken not merely within the limits of domestic economy but also through the medium of foreign trade. The absorption capacity of foreign markets for the products of Soviet agriculture, Shanin stressed, was still far from being exhausted; and Sokol'nikov strongly protested the contention that the policy he was advocating precluded the quick industrialization of the country. Precisely the opposite was true:

Only by stimulating agricultural exports can we obtain during the next years an amount of foreign currency which will enable us to finance the importation of equipment as well as of raw materials for our industry and to accomplish reequipment and expansion, if we really want to catch up with the tempo and the scale of foreign industry. . . . Our industry would suffer only if we had gone too far in importing finished [consumers] goods from abroad. This would, in fact, narrow down the possibilities for the operation of our industry.*

Shanin was somewhat less outspoken on this point than Sokol'nikov. He never stated in so many words what kind of imported industrial products should, in his view, receive priority — capital or consumers goods — although he did emphasize that the needs in the field of metals and machinery would have to be satisfied primarily by imports.[7] He was, however, quite explicit about the limits of the advocated line of action. An allowance had to be made, first of all, for military requirements. Economic calculation might show that a big transfer of resources from agriculture to industry would bring best results when undertaken, say, after ten years; but if the armed intervention from abroad (which was for Shanin, as well as for the other participants of the debate, a virtual certainty) could be reasonably expected to occur after five years, it was clearly imperative to deviate from the optimal pattern and to set the date of the shift so as to maximize industrial growth within the relevant five year period. Aside from this extraneous constraint, there was still a qualification inherent in the logic of the policy itself. The "cheapest expansion of the national economy" could not last forever: "One cannot believe that the world market is unlimited for all lines of our agriculture."[8] Finally, there

* VKP, *XIV s'ezd*, p. 331. It was not clear by what means Sokol'nikov intended to achieve the increase in agricultural exports. In the same speech he lashed out violently against Bukharin's "get rich" slogan and sided with the Left in its critique of too conciliatory a policy toward the rich peasants who produced at that time a large part of the marketable surplus of Soviet agriculture. This was not, of course, a very consistent position.

was an allowance for the "infant industry" consideration: the need for protection was granted in cases when "[relative] dearness is attributable only to the initial period of operation." [9]

But neither of these factors involved a serious modification of the ingenious scheme. Military necessities would hasten the shift toward industry, but the basic rule for choosing the appropriate moment for this shift would still hold within the shortened time period. Besides, it was pointed out that an overambitious military buildup could seriously impair the efficiency of the economy which would boomerang against defense; and that the importance of the "good will" of the peasants, with its implications for food supply and for the morale of the population, had to be weighed against the need for speed in armament production. Similarly, the exhaustion of foreign outlets for the growing surpluses of Soviet grain would mean merely that reshuffling toward other lines would set in earlier and be more gradual than otherwise. The reference to the infant industry argument, finally, did not amount to much as long as the time horizon of the "protected" investment was left undetermined and the wider repercussions it was bound to have were not brought in. Consequently, the underlying principle for determining the sequence of production lines to which the main emphasis had to be successively awarded would remain the same. A high rate of profit resulting from low capital intensity; easy convertibility into industrial supplies via foreign trade; proximity to agriculture which was assumed to remain the basis of the national economy for a long time to come — these were still the criteria for priority, although the answers read off the slide rule would be gradually changing:

After the world market [for agricultural goods] is exhausted in its direct form, it should be reopened through the industrial processing of agricultural raw material (sugar, alcohol, textiles).

. . . After these outlets, too, are exhausted, development should continue primarily along the lines of industry working for the home market but utilizing agricultural raw material or, at least, agricultural food supply. At the same time we must develop also the industries which are not processing agricultural raw material but are important for exportation purposes. . . .[10]

At each of these stages expansion would be more "expensive" than at the preceding one, since the capital requirements per unit of output would grow. But this increasing cost would be bearable and worth incurring because the Soviet economy would have built up in the meanwhile considerable stocks by giving priority to the right kind of investment and by making full use of the comparative advantages in international trade. This would, in Shanin's view, conform to the normal pattern of the development of backward regions:

A number of countries in process of industrialization were starting with light industry, importing industrial semifinished goods and most up-to-date equipment at low prices from the more advanced countries, and were in such a way promoting at small cost development of their light industry. Only after these lines had accumulated sufficient reserves of commodities which could be thrown in for building-up subsequent industry lines (heavy industry), was it possible to start development of the latter. . . .[11]

◻

One might perhaps define the place of Shanin's and Sokol'nikov's contribution in the debate by saying that they tried in effect to repeat Lenin's performance of 1921 on a different plane. The architect of the NEP wanted to start the economy on the road to recovery by opening up the trade between small-scale industry and peasant farming and by letting the rest of the system partake of the resulting benefits. To the most moderate of his disciples small-scale production was to serve as the tugboat of the whole economy not only in reactivating the idle productive capacity but also in promoting long-range development. The argument Shanin put forward in support of this case left little to be desired from the viewpoint of internal consistency and explicitness. It was equally obvious that his description of the new elements in the economic situation was plausible as far as it went. As we will see later, however, it covered only a part of the ground; and it will be shown that particular elements of the analysis as well as Shanin's ultimate conclusions were open to gravest doubt. Yet the general reaction to these ideas was (with a few exceptions) not an attempt to probe into the weak spots of the argument, but a shocked silence interrupted by sporadic name-calling. The Shanin-Sokol'nikov conception may have been one of the lineal descendants of O prodnaloge, but it was surely the least appreciated member of the family. Besides, at the time it was born, another and more formidable attack against the official policy was already in full swing.

In a sense, Bukharin had been on the defensive from the very beginning. When he blasted the evils of monopoly or warned of grave dangers to the "workers-peasant bloc" he was not shooting at an imaginary opponent, but at a very real and resourceful adversary. This was Evgeni A. Preobrazhenski who had been Bukharin's comrade-in-arms in the latter's Left Communist period and who was now the chief economic theorist of the renascent left opposition, led by Trotsky. It was not surprising that the challenge to the "ideology of the restoration period" came from this side. The left-wing Communists wanted to solve the harrowing problems of a socialist regime in a backward Russia, faced with advanced capitalist countries, by aiming at a resumption of all-out revolutionary action in the West and at the rapid growth of the industrial proletariat at home. The less chance the first part of the blueprint had in the immediate future, the stronger was the emphasis put on the second. The time had come, it was felt, to turn the tables against the "private sector," first of all against the peasantry which had imposed upon the Soviet regime the retreat toward the "mixed economy" of the NEP and which was certain to bring about a full-scale restoration of capitalism unless drastically reduced in its social and economic weight. The task consisted in stating the case not in terms of wishful thinking or nostalgic longing for the "heroic period of the Russian revolution" but in the language of present-day realities and necessities. This was precisely what Preobrazhenski attempted to do in his *Novaya ekonomika* which came out in 1926. The main chapter of this book, however, had already appeared in late 1924 and had immediately drawn Bukharin's angry rebuttal.

□

The goods famine of the winter of 1925 held the same place of honor in Preobrazhenski's argument as the "scissors crisis" of 1923 did in Bukharin's. In this respect his point of departure resembled that of Shanin. Unlike the official spokesmen of the party and government, Preobrazhenski did not ascribe the whole disturbance to the lack of foresight on the part of industrial management or of the banking authorities. The inflationary trouble of 1925 was to him an accentuated expression of deep-seated maladjustments in the structure of Soviet economy.

In his view, the shortages of the present were, to a large extent, the results of the enforced prodigality of the past. In the period of War Communism normal capital formation was interrupted: "We did not accumulate — the best thing we could do was to use up our resources as economically as possible." [12] The process continued in the early years of NEP either in the form of an all-out "auction sale" of industrial commodities regardless of cost, or by the use of amortization quotas for the purpose of wage increases and replenishment of stocks.

This policy undoubtedly had had immediate effects which were beneficial. It had kept the city population and the armies in the field from starving during the Civil War and it had permitted a great increase in output in the early years of the NEP: "The consumption of fixed capital constituted an advantage at this time because fixed capital and stocks of raw material would be a dead weight if labor had not transformed them into consumers' goods." [13] But as time went by the less attractive aspects of such a procedure were bound to reveal themselves. The reserve of minor and relatively inexpensive improvements would be gradually worked off: "The possibilities of the rationalization of production within the framework of the old technology are approaching exhaustion." [14] Moreover, the possibility of securing output increases by more intensive use of existing facilities was diminishing as capacity limits were drawing closer.[15] Since the capital stock had been reduced in size by years of underreplacement, this amounted to saying that the recovery was bound to stop short of the prewar level. (Preobrazhenski might have pointed out that, for reasons to be discussed later, an actual downturn was not impossible.) In order to prevent this from happening, the long overdue renewal of plant was to be carried through in a short span of time. This "bunched" replacement would clearly require a drastic increase in the volume of investment.

The situation as Preobrazhenski saw it, however, called for something much more far-reaching. This was due in part to the fact that such an extensive renewal of equipment provided the best opportunity for a wide-scale application of the technological improvements which had accumulated over the life time of the old plant and which involved a higher amount of capital per head.* Another, and no less compelling reason for advancing beyond "maintaining the capital intact" at its original level lay in the circumstance that the impact of revolutionary change had upset the precarious equilibrium of the Russian economy not only from the side of supply but also from that of demand. The share of industrial labor in national income had increased: "Our present wages are determined to a lesser extent than before the war by the value of labor power and in the future will be even less determined by it." [16] Of still greater portent, however, was the transformation in the status of the peasantry. In Tsarist Russia a large portion of the income originating in peasant agriculture was absorbed by payments to the government and landlords. In order to get the money for the fulfillment of these obligations, the peasant had to sell a corresponding part of his produce without buying anything in return. This had a twofold effect. On the one hand, a relatively large marketable surplus of agricultural goods was provided; on the other, the claims of the great majority of the population upon industrial output were reduced by the sum total of these "forced sales." The amount deducted from peasant income was undoubtedly respent in the main. This reexpenditure, however, absorbed a smaller share of domestic output than a corresponding amount of peasant spending would have done; a large part of it (to-

---

* Preobrazhenski described this situation very succinctly several years later when he argued that "the renewal of fixed capital in conditions of rapid technological progress inevitably transforms itself into an increase in the total amount of fixed capital as a result of the increase in the organic composition of capital in general." (*Zakat kapitalizma* [Leningrad, 1931], p. 83.) True, this statement referred to developments under capitalism, but Preobrazhenski undoubtedly held it to be valid also with regard to the Soviet economy of the twenties when he spoke of the possibility of "amortizing the old fixed capital which is technologically backward, and substituting gradually for it the technologically superior one" (*Novaya ekonomika*, p. 32), and when he insisted that technological progress under capitalism as well as under socialism involves "as a rule" a rise in the organic composition of capital (p. 207).

gether with a sizeable fraction of industrial profits) went abroad either to service the foreign debt or as payment for imported luxury consumption goods, while its physical counterpart was exported. The October Revolution put an end to the old system. Rent payments were wiped out and agricultural taxes amounted in 1924–1925 to less than one-third of the total peasant obligations before the war. The unstabilizing effects of this upheaval were momentous:

> Out of a given amount of the marketable output . . . a much smaller amount than before the war is going for forced sales; this means that the effective demand of the peasantry for industrial commodities and for the products of interpeasant exchange must correspondingly increase. . . . [Consequently] the stabilization of the relation between the total volume of the industrial and of the agricultural marketable output at the level of their prewar proportions implies a drastic disturbance in the equilibrium between the effective demand of the village and the marketable output of the town.[17]

The conclusion was clear — productive capacity had to increase over and above the prewar level in order to catch up with the increased effective demand. The failure to accomplish this would result in a recurrence of the goods famine a few years hence, just as the failure to make sufficient provision for capital maintenance in the past made inevitable the present goods famine. This was the point at which Preobrazhenski hammered incessantly from this time on.

The explosive possibilities of the situation were further aggravated by another effect of the changed income structure upon peasant behavior. The reduction in the burden of compulsory payments not only increased the peasant demand for city products at a given level of the agricultural marketable surplus, but it also influenced decisively the volume of this surplus by making it to a much greater extent dependent upon the peasants' willingness to trade. This was what Preobrazhenski had in mind when he stated that "as a result of the decrease in forced sales the peasantry now enjoys a much greater freedom in the choice of the time and of the terms at which to dispose of its own surpluses." He was even more explicit when he added that "the peasants are nowadays in no hurry to sell grain." And while he failed to spell out the immediate implications of this state of affairs, they were both unmistakable and ominous. The average peasant might have been willing to market the same total amount of his produce as before the war if the decrease in compulsory payments had enabled him to buy more in return. Since what he could actually get from the city was by now probably less than before the revolution, it was only logical for him to keep his sales below the prewar level and to divert the difference toward his own consumption as well as to livestock feeding, lending to poorer peasants, or plain hoarding. The dissatisfaction of the peasants need not, moreover, express itself in economic noncooperation alone. It might, as at the end of the Civil War, find its outlet in political discontent, culminating in open rebellion:

If this system does not satisfy a certain minimum of wants, we shall have systematic underproduction and insufficient satisfaction of effective demand; this can influence the mood of the masses and can result in what Comrade Lenin warned us against more than once: the masses will think of a system which would better satisfy their wants. Here lies the greatest danger and that is why we are so anxious about the volume of investment.[18]

Once again, it was the excess demand rather than deficient demand which was the chief villain in the piece.

■

Considerations of this kind were in the forefront of Preobrazhenski's argument. Yet they were, naturally enough, not the only points in the case for a sustained high rate of expansion. The description of the specific nature of the inflationary pressures which had been set off by the postwar changes was supplemented by observations on the structure of the economy exposed to these pressures, and by a statement of the long-run objectives to be achieved. Some of the latter, as one would expect, revolved around purely political issues such as the requirements of defense, with Preobrazhenski and his fellow leftists taking a more dramatic view of the imminence of war than the rest. Such points were argued with great vehemence, and the underlying anxieties undoubtedly played an important role in the ultimate motivations:

Each of us knows full well that we must build socialism, are building it and shall build it. We should know, however, that we won't be given much time to build. We should expect a drive of rich peasantry united with the world capital which will start an economic as well as a military-political offensive. . . . We are building socialism in a situation of a breathing spell between two battles.[19]

But on the level of analysis such fears were distinctly secondary when compared with the arguments of a different type to which we shall now turn.

As one of the basic "conditions of equilibrium" of the Soviet economy, Preobrazhenski listed "the gradual absorption of the surplus population of the country." [20] He never went into extensive characterization of this phenomenon except for noting that it had been inherited by the Soviet economy from the agrarian structure of the old regime and that the labor-displacing effects of technological and organizational improvements for which the backwardness of the country left ample room made the task of absorption more difficult.[21] Neither did he attempt to establish a link between the surplus population and the goods famine by showing how deeply imbedded the inflationary tendencies of an economy are when its equipment, apart from several years' depletion, is a bottleneck for the utilization of the labor force. He did, however, refer to another aspect of the same problem, when he pointed out that the peasants' ability to fall back upon the production of nonfarm goods in their own households, and thus "to bypass the state industry" in response to high prices of its products is greatly enhanced by the existence of "huge disguised unemployment in the countryside." [22] His conclusion was stated emphatically: "All attempts to solve the unemployment problem in a radical way lead to the problem of accumulation." [23] Rapid industrialization, spearheaded by the expansion of the capital-goods sector, draws away a large part of surplus labor from the land. At the same time it counteracts the displacement effect of labor-saving innovation:

> The whole process of the rationalization of labor won't lead to stagnation in the business of expanding the cadres of the labor force employed in the state-owned industry only if it is over-compensated by the sufficiently rapid expansion of the industrial basis of the country in absolute terms. And this rapid expansion calls for a much more rapid accumulation in the industry than we have at the moment. [24]

Preobrazhenski did not deny that the problem of the rural surplus population could and should be tackled also in a more direct way, namely, by promoting the intensification of agriculture, "the possibility of which is directly proportional to our backwardness in comparison with the foreign farming." However, he qualified this admission by insisting that a considerable increase in the rate of accumulation in agriculture which such intensification would inevitably involve should not be pressed forward "at the expense of that part of the surplus fund which the village gives to the city for the purpose of the socialist reconstruction." [25] The expansion of the industry which constituted "the key to the future solution of all basic problems of the period of transition" would be slowed down thereby. This would, in his view, inevitably backfire upon agriculture. It would, in the first place, check the increase in the supply of industrial goods and thus deprive the peasant of the most powerful stimulus to intensify his own production. And it would also limit the opportunities for improvement in efficiency of the peasant farming, predicated upon the development of "external economies" and most certainly arrest the process of modernization by intensive reequipment.

The expanded production in industry, its sufficiently quick tempo, the development of railway networks, canals, electrification, etc., are indispensable also for the peasant economy which cannot without the assistance of a growing industry develop its productive forces even though small-scale production, let alone advance toward the level of productive cooperation.[26]

He goes on to put the case even more strongly: "Only when industry can stand on a new technological basis, will the stream of values from the city to the countryside along the channels of long-term credit become a torrential flow." [27]

It is not difficult to discover a basic assumption which underlies the reasoning of the preceding paragraph and which we have encountered in an earlier context: the "new technological basis" is consistently taken to mean the rapid spread of technology requiring a higher amount of capital per head. It is this proposition which makes unemployment serve as an even more forceful argument in favor of a high rate of capital construction. A community attempting to provide tools for its unemployed members at a faster rate than before must, other things being equal, show an increase in the share of capital goods in its total output; and the higher the capital intensity of the new plant, the stronger this increase must necessarily be.

To these considerations Preobrazhenski added another which was less obvious, and which referred to another specific characteristic of capitalistic technology. He argued, in effect, that not only must investment, in a modern economy, increase in relation to the consumption of the given period if a discontinuous increase in the final output of a subsequent period is to be achieved, but that the output of investment goods must increase by an amount equal to the multiple of the accretion to the final output they are expected to produce: "In order to increase the annual output of consumers goods in light industry by, say, 100 million rubles, the output of the means of production must increase by 400 to 500 million rubles in the preceding period." * There is, he was quick to add, an important exception to this rule. If unutilized capacity is in existence as in the first period of NEP in the Soviet Union, the output can expand for a while without any significant increase in the construction of additional equipment, and can outstrip in its rate of growth the increase in new investment which would be confined primarily to building up the working capital.[28] When the capacity reserve is exhausted, however, any further increase in the level of output is predicated upon a still greater upward jump in the volume of investment in fixed capital. This investment, moreover, while requiring a larger amount of resources than in the previous situation, will show its first effects at a more distant date, since it takes time to build the fixed capital as well as to use it up. "The new plants will begin to produce three or four years after the start of their construction; this is the result more of a technological than of an economic necessity." [29]

The crucial importance of these peculiarities of modern equipment for Preobrazhenski's case is evident. They put teeth into his argument that the addition to the capital stock must be large. They explain his insistence that the expansion of productive capacity must start well in advance of the time when the limit for increase in the utilization of the

* VKA, XXII (1927), p. 41. Preobrazhenski did not complete the argument to show that while the rate of increase in output equals the ratio of the increment in equipment to the total capital stock, the rate of increase in investment equals the ratio of this increment to an investment volume which is a fraction of the capital stock.

existing equipment is reached, if the new plants are to step into the gap promptly and prevent a goods famine from developing. But could not the weight of these factors be lessened by spreading over time the reconstruction of equipment through tackling separate tasks successively in the order of their relative urgency? The coincidence of "reconstruction" with long overdue replacement goes a long way toward explaining why the satisfaction of the "bunched" investment demand could not in this particular case be extended too liberally without penalty of further shrinkage. Preobrazhenski implicitly advanced another reason when he stated that the required accumulation must be sufficient "to secure the development of the whole complex of the state economy, not only of its particular parts, because the chain connection in the movement of the whole complex makes an isolated advance entirely impossible." [30]

This could be interpreted as a reference to the phenomenon of complementarity between industries which has since the late twenties commanded the increasing attention of prominent Western economists such as Allyn A. Young, P. N. Rosenstein-Rodan, and Ragnar Nurkse, and which has been used, in conjunction with "indivisibility" considerations, as a case in point for a high volume of investment in the initial stages of the economic development of backward areas.[31] Preobrazhenski, however, did not pursue this idea any further, and it is difficult to say on the basis of his brief remark how much weight he assigned to it — especially since two different lines of argument converge at this point. This appears from the sentence which immediately follows the passage quoted: the "chain connection in the movement of the whole complex" is contrasted with the "method of capitalist guerrilla warfare, private initiative and competition" which characterized the expansion both of early "manufacture" and of modern factory production.

Apparently, the necessity of expanding simultaneously

along a broad front is tied in with the socialist character of the economy. Less clear, however, is the precise nature of this connection. Is it intended to mean that the collective form of ownership makes possible the application of a higher type of technology than is possible under capitalism? Or does the causal relationship run the opposite way, namely, that the system of centralized over-all planning (which was to Preobrazhenski as well as to his fellow debaters the only consistent form of socialist economy) cannot operate efficiently and prove itself superior to capitalism without a high level of integration and concentration in the structure of production which assumes, in turn, a higher degree and wider spread of large-scale technology than under capitalism? Or, finally, is the greater accumulation, to a certain extent, a kind of protective cushion for state enterprise, necessary as a result of its temporary inferiority in efficiency as compared with foreign and domestic private competitors?

One could find in the *Novaya ekonomika* material to support each of these alternative explanations, with arguments of the third type receiving the strongest emphasis. This may seem a typical case of putting ideological allegiances above considerations of efficiency. Actually there was more to it, as we shall see later. At this point it suffices merely to take note of Preobrazhenski's position which, whatever its validity, leads straight to the heart of his ultimate policy recommendations.

If the irreducible minimum of capital requirements was as large as is indicated by all the foregoing, the question of securing the means clearly assumed paramount importance. Preobrazhenski provided the answer by an historical analogy. The productive powers of modern technology permitted the capitalism of the nineteenth century to finance its powerful expansion primarily out of the profits earned under conditions of unrestricted competition and to eliminate the smaller fry by the "artillery of cheap prices." The possibility of applying this technology, however, depended on a large accumulation of wealth and the availability of a free labor force. And since both these preconditions of the technological superiority of modern capitalism had to be created, obviously enough, before the superiority existed, they could never have come into being if the rules of the competitive game had been adhered to from the start. A number of institutional changes had first to be made. The relative "autarky" of the primitive peasant economies had to be broken and their participants forced into the market; the independent precapitalist producers had to be either separated from their means of production or at least deprived of a part of the product of their labor. In order to achieve this, there had to be set into motion a whole array of highly illiberal techniques, ranging from the outright compulsion of enclosures and workhouses, through taxation and state-protected manipulation of prices in the domestic and international markets, to the inflationist devaluation of money. This formative period of modern capitalism was called by Marx the epoch of "primitive capitalist accumulation." It had now to find its counterpart in "primitive socialist accumulation," * which was to serve as a midwife for the socialist society of the future.

Understandably such an analogy was bound to cause a great stir in Preobrazhenski's audience. For generations Marxian socialists had been using the famous Part VIII of the first volume of *Capital* not only as a contribution to the understanding of economic history but as a powerful means

---

* Preobrazhenski was not the originator of this term which made him famous. In his earlier book, *Bumazhnye den'gi v epokhu proletarskoi diktatury* (Moscow, 1920), where he used it for the first time, he gave credit for this "excellent expression" to V. M. Smirnov, a well-known Soviet economist who was later closely associated with Preobrazhenski in the left-wing opposition.

of arousing the minds of men against a system which "comes dripping from head to foot, from every pore, with blood and dirt." Actually, Preobrazhenski advocated neither the application of methods of violence against the nonsocialist small-scale producers nor the elevation of one group of society (industrial workers) to the rank of a newly privileged stratum, although no less an opponent than Bukharin accused him of aiming at the second.

For one who liked strong medicine in argumentation as well as in policies, the analogy with the period of primitive capitalist accumulation served merely to provide a dramatic illustration for his idea that the "law of value," which governs the operation of the competitive market and makes the exchange ratio between goods depend on the relative amounts of "socially necessary labor" contained in them, had to be suppressed as far as possible. "An exchange of the smaller quantum of labor of one economic system (socialism) for the greater quantum of labor of another economic system (capitalism)" [32] had to be secured instead if a rapid advance from a low initial level were to be made. This was what the famous "law of primitive socialist accumulation" actually amounted to. It stood for the whole set of devices which in various ways served one purpose — to bring about "within the limits of what is economically possible and technically feasible" [33] a shift of productive resources from the private to the socialized sector over and above the share the latter could obtain as a result of the operation of the law of value in a competitive market.

The necessity for counteracting the "law of value" applied first of all to the sphere of the foreign relations of the Soviet economy. One of the crucial differences between capitalist and socialist primitive accumulation lay in the comparative efficiency of the regions in which the new system was in ascendancy and those still dominated by the old. The countries where capitalism had an early start had a definite lead over the rest of the world in terms of economic power. The socialized sector of the Soviet economy was far behind the industries of America and Western Europe. Preobrazhenski was fully aware that this difference need not be entirely to the disadvantage of the young socialist system if purely economic considerations should prevail. Indeed, every single basic difficulty of the Soviet economy would, according to him, be much less formidable in a smoothly operating system of international trade and foreign lending. With regard to direct investment, Preobrazhenski was rather apprehensive. He feared that "concessions" could, if permitted to develop on a large scale, become dangerous to the state-owned industry, primarily because they would provide a striking demonstration of the economic superiority of mature capitalism over the newly-born socialism of a backward country. Yet he was strongly in favor of foreign loans, and was prepared to let them bear interest at a rate above the normal. The burden of such payment, he argued, "would certainly be much less than the new values which would be added to the fund of socialist accumulation." And he minced no words in stating the reasons for this view:

The long-term foreign loan is, on the one hand, one of the ways in which foreign capital exploits the new young economy. But, on the other hand, it can accelerate the process of socialist accumulation in a most powerful fashion. It represents a once-over discontinuous increase in the fund of socialist accumulation, it accelerates the process of the technological reequipment of the state economy and, consequently, it shortens the period that the state industry has to stay in the preschool grade of socialism. It creates possibilities for employing many tens of thousands of unemployed workers who are now separated from production owing to the lack of the material elements of production in the hands of the state, and thereby transforms these unemployed into participants of the socialist accumulation. . . .[34]

The trouble consisted in the fact that even such bait would not bring about the desired result because "foreign capital does not intend to flow into an alien economic system on a large scale." [35] The Soviet economy had therefore to bear the full burden of its own reequipment, and to set its rate of accumulation at a correspondingly high level: "If the [world] law [of value] had been operating smoothly, such an accumulation in conditions of overindustrialization of Europe would be entirely nonsensical." [36] This did not mean that the whole job was to be done by the domestic investment-goods industries. Preobrazhenski was emphatic in insisting upon the "protection, development, and creation of particular lines of means of production," [37] which would not survive in a free trial of strength with their foreign competitors but which had a real chance for improvement in the future. But he was at the same time careful not to press this point too far. He did not explicitly restate the argument of Trotsky according to which a country whose industrial structure (inherited from the past) permitted it to satisfy only a minor part of its capital requirements by domestic production could not attempt to attain a much larger degree of self-sufficiency in this field within the span of a few years without running into heavy trouble.[38] He expressed the same idea in a more general form, however, when he emphasized the necessity of weighing the infant industry considerations against the benefits to be secured from the "attempt to make the best possible use of the world division of labor, i.e., to import more of those machines whose domestic production is less advantageous under existing economic conditions." [39] Such a policy would not merely mean a gain in the efficiency of expansion but, what was somewhat less obvious, a gain in speed. The Soviet economy would have to give up, at the most, an amount of current consumption equivalent to the volume of the annual inflow of the importable equipment and not to the amount of the total stock of capital (with all supplementary subsidiaries) which would be needed to produce the given volume at home.*

The next step consisted in setting free for these capital-goods supplies the largest possible part of the proceeds of current exports. This was actually the major aim of the "socialist protectionism" as advocated by Preobrazhenski, although he did not always make it quite clear. His often-repeated warnings that two-thirds to three-quarters of the Soviet large-scale industry would be forced to shut down in the event of unrestricted imports seemed too sweeping in view of his own statements about the goods famine and the insatiable demand for equipment. No doubt, some domestic industries would be seriously threatened even in conditions of repressed inflation. But to the extent that these lines were worth preserving for valid "infant industry" reasons, a modicum of tariff protection or of subsidization would be sufficient, and the ruthless use of the foreign trade monopoly would seem like too drastic a device. Yet, the main peril about which Preobrazhenski was concerned consisted not in the possible effects of foreign competition but in the certainty that an adjustment of the composition of foreign supplies to the voluntary preferences of the population would reduce the amount of capital goods to a level which would imply stagnation, if not actual capital consumption under the specific conditions of the Soviet industry of that period. In order to stave off this danger, the foreign

* This seems, in fact, to be the meaning of the following somewhat unwieldy passage: "Heavy industry [does not have to] wait for its own deficit in the means of production to be covered by its own expansion, and for the new plants to be equipped with machines produced by itself; this would greatly delay the moment of putting these plans into operation and prolong the crisis within Department I itself as well as in its exchange relationship with Department II. . . . [Instead, it] cuts through the dilemma by importing the equipment which, if produced at home, would . . . divert the insufficient accumulation towards plants, the production of which, in view of the connection with the world economy, could easily be postponed." (VKA, XXII [1927], pp. 46–47.)

trade monopoly had to be used consistently for securing an indisputable priority of replacement and expansion needs in the total volume of Soviet imports. The reintegration of the Soviet economy in the system of the world division of labor would then be secured and a shift of resources from Western capitalism toward Soviet socialism would be achieved, with the domestic private sector footing the bill:

We are accumulating at prices which are twice as high as the foreign only because we are, as a result of our struggle against the law of value, forcibly attaching the domestic market to our technologically backward industry while the exported goods of the peasant economy are being sold at world market prices and the import program is subordinated to the task of the accumulation of fixed capital and the replenishment of stocks of circulating capital.[40]

The domestic situation presented essentially the same problems. The efficiency relationship between the old and the new system was also here the reverse of that prevailing in the formative period of capitalism. The state-owned plants had "no individual superiority with regard to the plants of an historically lower stage."[41] This relative weakness of the nationalized large-scale industry was mainly a result of the long period of economic shrinkage which had hurt the large plants more than the small. With the gradual elimination of bottlenecks restricting capacity utilization, the restoration of labor discipline in factories, and the making good of arrears in the maintenance of equipment, the relationship was certain to be reversed. But even such "filling-in" could not be successfully carried out on the basis of the gross savings which industry could make under competitive conditions. It was even less realistic to expect that such interindustrial accumulation would be sufficient to sustain an expansion at anything like the high rate envisaged, particularly since the methods of the ruthless exploitation of labor which had raised profits in the days of the Industrial Revolution were now ruled out. "The victorious working class . . . cannot treat its own labor power, its health and working conditions in the same way as capitalism did; this is a definite barrier to socialist accumulation." [42] Such a policy, moreover, would not be merely in conflict with the notions of equity. It would be bad on grounds of efficiency as well. "The increase in real wages is made indispensable by the very fact of the industrialization of the country since the change in the technological basis of the whole state economy . . . inevitably demands an increase in the skills of the workers." [43]

Imports of foreign equipment, although highly valuable, were obviously insufficient for bridging the gap between requirements and availabilities. The most heroic efforts of "socialist protectionism" could not go beyond the limits set by export surpluses consisting largely of agricultural goods, and the volume and price of these were determined outside the sphere of the direct control of the state. The importance of the protectionist trade policy, however, consisted not merely in transforming a certain quantum of domestic consumers goods into a corresponding amount of foreign equipment, but also in its function as flank protection for even more drastic measures against the "law of value" in the domestic sphere. The effective curbs against foreign competition would strengthen the monopolistic controls at home. This proposition of the Marxist theory of imperialism applied, according to Preobrazhenski, to the Soviet economy as well. The latter, moreover, could avail itself of the opportunity offered to a much greater extent than a system based upon private ownership of the means of production: "The concentration of the whole of the big industries of the country in the hands of a single trust, that is, in the hands of the workers' state, increases to an extraordinary extent in comparison with monopolistic capitalism the possibility of carrying out . . . a price policy on the basis of monopoly."

The price determined in such a way is in fact nothing but "another form of the taxation of private production." [44]

Preobrazhenski did not, to be sure, renounce direct taxation as an instrument of the redistribution of income in favor of socialist industry. In fact, he definitely wanted it to be used together with discriminatory measures in the field of railway rates, credit, and the like.* Taxation through price, however, was in his view the most effective single device — both because of the "extreme convenience of collection which did not require a penny for a special fiscal apparatus" and for reasons of political expediency. "The way of direct taxation is the most dangerous way, leading to a break with the peasants." [45]

It would be wrong to assume that Preobrazhenski ignored the limitations of the method he was advocating. On the contrary, he was quite explicit about them when he stated that "the state is free to determine prices (at any point) within a range from the cost level to the exhaustion of the whole effective demand (*taking into account, of course, the influence of prices upon demand*)." [46] Pushing price increases too far would defeat their purpose and result either in "the emergence of competing [private] enterprises with lower costs per unit than in the state enterprises" or in "a shrinking demand and direct refusal to buy" as during the "scissors crisis" of 1923.[47] Also the monopoly of foreign trade was to him a potential source of serious, if less immediate, internal

---

* In the earlier period Preobrazhenski had gone on record as an ardent advocate of still another method of promoting "socialist primitive accumulation." The already mentioned *Bumazhnye den'gi*, known for its much-quoted panegyric on the printing press as that "machine gun which attacked the bourgeois regime in the rear," contained an analysis of inflationary money printing as a form of taxation. But while he made a specific reference to this device in *Novaya ekonomika* as an important tool of policy in the past, he refrained from recommending its use in the present; and in his later pronouncements he took pains to stress that a fall in the value of the ruble could cause severe disruption of the economy, climaxed by a massive withdrawal of peasants from the market.

friction. Indeed, his fears for the stability of the Soviet system were largely a reflection of the grave view he took of the peasants' resentment against the devious manipulation which deprived them of those cheap foreign goods they actually wanted to have in return for the exported products of their labor, and raised against them the prices of domestic industrial output. It is this attitude, incidentally, which explains why the defense considerations were rather less central to the leftists' case for rapid industrialization than to the argument of their opponents, although offhand one would be inclined to assume the opposite. The representatives of the official party line as well as Shanin viewed the possibility of armed aggression as the main danger implied in the coexistence of a socialist Russia and a capitalist world. This was the chief reason for them to step up the rate of capital construction above the level which they considered optimal, had this "encirclement" not existed. To Preobrazhenski and his friends the low productivity of the Soviet industry with regard to the West and the implied sacrifices of the population were a menace which would become deadly for the Soviet system even without military intervention from abroad. The investment tempo had to be raised accordingly in order to provide not only for more "guns" but also for more "butter" in a not-too-distant future, if *this* kind of external danger were to be met.

These were the resistances to be reckoned with. But "primitive socialist accumulation" could be relied upon to soften these resistances by its long-run effects. The improved and enlarged equipment resulting from the operation of this policy would raise the income of the whole society, including the peasants. The latter would consequently demand more industrial goods despite the fact that the prices of these goods, while declining gradually toward the world market price level, would be prevented from falling to the full extent of the reduction in unit costs. In this way, an

increase in real income through time would be paralleled
by an increase in the effectiveness of the monopolistic
squeeze and result in a steadily growing movement of resources into investment in industrial construction. The
process would continue until the productive capacity of
the Soviet economy reached a level where "technological
and economic superiority over capitalism" [48] could be secured. The monopolistic techniques could then be dispensed
with and further expansion would proceed exclusively on
the basis of the "surplus product" originating within the
socialized sector. This, in turn, would set the stage for an
even more momentous change. The accumulation drive
would have to recede into the background and give way
to the "satisfaction of the wants of the participants of collective production," [49] as the guiding force of the economic
policy. The "cycle of transformation of the whole economy"
would therewith be completed.

◘

The appearance of the main chapter of the *Novaya
ekonomika* evoked heated polemics, which reached new
heights after the publication of the book and continued
unabated for years. The critics, insofar as they were concerned not with political underpinnings but with economic
reasoning, aimed first of all, at Preobrazhenski's concept
of "two laws" as a proposition in the theory and policy of
socialist pricing. At first sight the discussion in this field
seemed to be a quibble about words. Some of the opponents
simply objected to the idea that the Soviet economy might
have more than one set of ruling principles, without any
serious attempt to support such protests with articulate
arguments. Others admitted the existence of the conflicting
"two regulators" but preferred to put it in the traditional
way by contrasting "market" and "planning" despite Preobrazhenski's insistence that such a procedure is devoid of

any meaning unless what is being planned for and how the market operates is made explicit. They entertained no doubts that as long as goods are being sold for money and not assigned directly to the consumers, the "law of value" must hold. The obvious objection that this is true (according to Marx) only under conditions of the unrestricted movement of factors and goods, was in their view adequately met by the admission that the law of value is operating in a "garbled" way when such free movement does not exist.

Whenever the controversy descended to concrete problems of policy, the element of semantics receded, and the argument gained in substance. For a Western student it is not difficult to recognize that some of the instances of the suspension of the "law of value" given by Preobrazhenski could, in principle, make good sense from the viewpoint of modern theory. They could easily come under such familiar headings as "letting bygones be bygones," divergences between current and future costs, or social benefits versus private benefits. While the problem of choice between the manipulation of price and the application of a subsidy (or of a tax) was not raised in the debate with regard to discrepancies of this "microeconomic" type, it did come up when larger issues were discussed. Preobrazhenski, it will be remembered, favored the marking up of prices as the best way of redistributing income; his critics preferred the method of direct taxation. It would, nevertheless, be wrong to exaggerate the differences on this score. Preobrazhenski did not propose to rely exclusively upon taxation through price, nor were his opponents welfare economists in disguise. Bukharin, as we saw before, explicitly admitted the need for an upward "deviation" in the prices of industrial commodities. On the other hand, when he argued that a monopolistic policy weakens the incentive for improvements in methods of production, Preobrazhenski did not disagree. Instead, he made a somewhat vague reference to the "consumers' pressure of the working class on its state" which in conjunction with the less friendly pressure coming from the peasantry and foreign capital, could be relied upon to provide powerful stimuli for increase in productivity;[50] and he did not budge from his repeatedly stated view that the high profits made possible by monopolistic price policy would provide the necessary means for the required capital outlays.

The reasons for the inconclusive drift in argument which characterized much of the debate could hardly be shown more clearly than in this polemical encounter. The major protagonists were not sufficiently explicit about (or aware of) the fundamental differences in approach between them. The Bukharin of 1924–1925 was thinking in terms of the fullest, most balanced and most efficient utilization of the existing productive potential when he discussed long-run as well as short-run developments. Preobrazhenski was concerned about the insufficiency of this potential even from the viewpoint of the smooth day-to-day operation of the economy. To be sure, he did not deny the existence of partial disproportions and the importance of incentives. But he saw these issues against the broader background of "systematic underproduction" which had its twin roots in the egalitarian redistribution of income and in the shortage of capital accentuated by many years of underreplacement. His analysis brought out the gravity of such an imbalance in an economy with industrial equipment inadequate to absorb the available labor reserves even prior to its depletion, with millions of subsistence farmers hanging on the market by the skin of their teeth and with foreign borrowing reduced to a trickle. With regard to such a "macroeconomic" disequilibrium mere reliance upon improvements in allocative efficiency would clearly not suffice. Only the imposition of forced saving could restore stability, in the short run, by bringing the aggregate demand into equilibrium with the available supply, and, in the longer run, by making possible an expansion in total capacity which would permit a more abundant supply in the future. And only then would tangible incentives for increased effort be provided.

The price policy Preobrazhenski advocated was to serve as a tool for such forced saving. All other effects it might have were of secondary importance to him. The crucial point was not the adequacy of this particular tool and not even the broader problem as to the extent to which it is possible to combine the manipulation of the propensity to consume by the state and the untrammeled working of the price mechanism. Could Preobrazhenski's investment program be enforced, no matter what economic devices were used for this purpose? This was the real question — and it was here that Preobrazhenski's ideas met the most decisive objections.

◫

Preobrazhenski castigated his opponents for their failure to break with the "ideology of the restoration period" which led them to extol the possibilities of expansion within the framework of the existing capacity. Yet his critics were right when they pointed out that his own policy recommendations reflected the influence of the same ideology.[51] Indeed, the method of extracting "forced savings" from the peasantry by the manipulation of prices could work reasonably well (despite occasional snarls) in a period when such "abnormal" profits had to finance inventory replenishment and the most urgent maintenance measures, and when payment for the sacrifice involved in high prices was forthcoming in the form of large and almost instantaneous increases in current output. None of these considerations held any longer in regard to the reconstruction period. The transition from patchwork to the construction of fixed equipment on a large scale involved a drastic increase in investment expenditures per unit of time as well as an extension of the time period between the input of factors and the emergence of the final output.

Preobrazhenski was fully aware of this state of affairs as well as of the specific aggravating circumstances implicit in the Soviet situation. If, during this extended period of waiting, one part of the existing equipment after another was bound to decline in productivity or to go out of service without being promptly replaced, the reasons were to be sought not only in the channeling of a large part of the resources into time-absorbing investment processes, but also in the insufficient provision for replacement in the past.

We will be facing natural consequences of a situation when the fixed capital of the country greatly reduced by the amortization gaps of the preceding years, is being rebuilt in conditions of limited connections with the world economy and of the general deficiency of the internal accumulation in the physical form of the means of production.[52]

The attempt to make good the resulting decline in current output by an intensified use of the serviceable equipment could yield very modest results because of the rapidly approaching capacity limits, and could succeed only at steeply increasing costs. Preobrazhenski did not mention this fact explicitly in reference to the Soviet economy but he did note it in a later discussion of developments under capitalism when he pointed out that an increase in output based upon an increase in the amount of labor alone is accompanied by "increasing labor values" as a result of making use of less efficient plant and inferior land.[53] The conclusion was therefore inevitable that while the large addition to the existing stock of capital could be expected to have most salutary effects on the supply situation in the future, the investment which was necessary for producing this addition was bound to make things worse for the time being. Preobrazhenski, in fact, said this quite explicitly when he stated that "a dis-

continuous reconstruction of fixed capital involves a shift of
so much means of production toward the production of
means of production, which will yield output only after a few
years, that thereby the increase of the consumption funds
of the society will be stopped." [54] He did not, however, add
the inevitable conclusion that the amount of consumption
goods per employed worker would decline.

In such a situation an uncontrolled economy could not
avoid a wage-price spiral; but neither would the "workers'
state" acting in accordance with Preobrazhenski's directives
be able to keep the wages down in order to prevent an inflation. The shift of the main burden of the sacrifice to the
nonindustrial population was the remaining alternative. This
was what Preobrazhenski actually proposed to do by his
policy of "primitive socialist accumulation." But it was he
who had insisted that the increase in the peasants' ability to
spend out of given income was the strongest single stimulant
to "nonautonomous" investment; more importantly, no one
stated more forcefully than he the ever-present danger of a
peasants' strike in view of the lag in industrial supply. Such
a danger could materialize during the "discontinuous reconstruction" when peasants were expected to give up more
of their produce than before, while not getting correspondingly more in return (or more likely getting less). Preobrazhenski's celebrated directive: "Take from the petty bourgeois producers more than capitalism did [but] out of a
[proportionally] still larger income," could hardly hold at
this particular juncture.* The "petty bourgeois producers"

---

* *Novaya ekonomika*, p. 100. It is possible, however, that Preobrazhenski
viewed this formula (which earned him a pat on the shoulder from
Bukharin) as applicable in the long run rather than in the short run. He
was quick to add that the larger income of the small producers "will be
secured by the rationalization of the whole economy of the country,
including the small-scale economy, on the basis of the industrialization
of the country [and] intensification of agriculture" (*ibid.*) Moreover, the
whole proposition should presumably be taken to refer to a rather advanced
stage of this "rationalization" — otherwise it would not be consistent with

could respond to the attempt at an increased squeeze by
withdrawing from the market, thus killing the industrial
expansion by cutting off the supplies of food and, indirectly,
of the foreign capital goods bought from the proceeds of
agricultural exports. Or else, by forcing the state to capitu-
late, they could impose an increase in food prices and let the
inflation start from this side. The cure would prove deadlier
than the disease; this was, in effect, the point Preobrazhenski's opponents were making.

Preobrazhenski struggled vainly for a way out of this
dilemma. He tried to minimize the danger of high industrial
prices by pointing out that the prevailing low wholesale
prices were of little or no benefit to the peasants in any
event. When the wholesale price does not reflect the real
scarcity situation, he argued, the private trader (on whom
the peasants had to rely to a greater extent than did the
city population) "corrects" the price in his own favor.[55]
To this his opponents replied that even if it were true that
the peasants would not suffer after the upward price adjustment, the workers would, and the inflationary pressure would
start from the side of wages. They argued, moreover, that
an attempt to squeeze profit margins in retail trade by raising wholesale prices would result either in shifting the increases in wholesale prices onto consumers, or in the disruption of the distribution apparatus; that is, unless the state
were able to create a large network of its own (or cooperative) trade establishments — a policy to which Preobrazhenski strongly objected. The extension of state expenditure to
this sphere would, he believed, inevitably develop at the
expense of investment devoted to the expansion of productive
capacity.[56] The call for the increased taxation of rich peasants
was met by the answer that this would aggravate the situation

what Preobrazhenski had to say about increase in effectiveness of the
"socialist monopolism" as a result of the early successes of the "primitive
socialist accumulation."

even more by causing a curtailment of marketable surpluses
— a development which would be particularly serious because an abundant supply of needed agricultural implements for the main body of the peasantry could not be
expected in the immediate future.

It is perhaps not accidental that in the last and most
systematic recorded statement of his position, Preobrazhenski
did not repeat these concrete proposals but limited himself
to restating the problem in all its ramifications. He concluded
that "the sum total of these contradictions shows how
strongly our development toward socialism is confronted
with the necessity of ending our socialist isolation, not only
for political but also for economic reasons, and of leaning
for support in the future on the material resources of other
socialist countries." [57] At worst, this amounted to an admission that all attempts to find a solution within the limits of
the isolated Soviet economy would be merely squaring the
circle. At best, this was a desperate effort to obtain tomorrow's stability at the expense of enormously increased
tensions today, without knowing too well how to withstand
them.

It was not difficult for Preobrazhenski's opponents to prove
that the "superindustrialist" way was leading to an impasse.
To show a flaw in his reasoning was quite a different matter.
Indeed, the main argument seemed ominously foolproof.
The high rate of growth appeared as a vital necessity and at
the same time as a threat. Granted the underlying assumptions, it was the case of a choice between mortal sickness and
virtually certain death on the operating table.

III

Attempt at Synthesis

U P TO this point we have watched the discussion unfold vigorously only to land in what seems to be a blind alley. The representatives of the two major divergent schools appear to have done such a thorough job of demolishing their opposite numbers that in the light of their argument the Soviet economy seemed to be trapped between the Scylla of doing too little and the Charybdis of doing too much. It was only natural that efforts were made to break out of this deadlock. The work of Vladimir A. Bazarov, one of the intellectual lights of the Bolshevik movement during its first decade, and later the leading nonparty economist of the Gosplan, was undoubtedly one of the most remarkable of such endeavors.

Bazarov did not try to blink at the unpalatable facts. On the contrary, his name became forever identified in subsequent discussions with the "theory of the levelling-off curve"; and this "theory" was nothing but a slightly formalized way of saying that an economy endowed with considerable reserves of idle capacity and basing its increase in output primarily on the more intensive utilization of the available plant will experience a gradual tapering-off in its rate of growth as it approaches full-capacity limits. This conclusion, it goes without saying, was entirely consonant with the diagnosis of the situation as provided by Shanin, on the one hand, and by Preobrazhenski on the other. Indeed, even a glance at Bazarov's survey of the nature of the Soviet economic difficulties shows practically all the basic elements already familiar to us. The difference in the elasticity of supply at various stages of the restoration process is strongly emphasized:

In contrast to the previous years, when we still had in reserve all the elements of production activity and when quite insignificant expenditures for replacing some small items were sufficient in order to set into motion large quantities of idle productive forces, the putting of a new piece of fixed capital into operation requires at present greater and steadily increasing efforts.[1]

The postponement of significant replacement activity in the early stages of recovery is cited as a main reason for a sharp discontinuity in the subsequent period:

If we had been able to use the resources (of the restoration period) for new construction in the industrial field . . . , new industrial plants which would be on the level of modern technology would make it possible both to increase the output significantly and to reduce considerably its cost as compared with our present factories with their extremely obsolete and worn-out equipment. In such a way the putting of newly constructed plants into operation would, despite the constant and even deteriorating cost coefficients in the old plants, provide a firm material basis for a systematic, not too fast, but steady, fulfillment of the policy of deflation.[2]

Actually, however,

. . . We are approaching the end of the restoration process without a significant preparation for the coming period of reconstruction. As a result, we will inevitably experience a considerable slowing down in the tempo of our economic growth. Indeed, we have to make at once great outlays of reconstruction while the results of this will have an effect on the development of productive forces only after a few years, when the newly-built plants start entering operation one after another.[3]

Finally, the explosive potentialities of this investment hump are shown to be compounded by the high rate of consumption characteristic of postrevolutionary Russian economy:

> Before the war . . . despite a very modest level of development of productive forces, if measured in absolute terms, the industrial output showed a constant tendency toward overproduction, toward expanding beyond the limits of extremely restricted effective demand of the bulk of the population. In the present "period of transition" our economic system is characterized by a precisely opposite contradiction between the effective demand of working masses which is increasing rather fast, and the growth of social productive forces which is insufficient for satisfying this demand. . . . The basic disproportion which prevents our economy from reaching equilibrium at (or near to) the prewar level lies precisely in this permanent lagging of social output behind social demand.[4]

Bazarov did not believe that this high propensity to consume could be substantially changed within the existing institutional framework. It was axiomatic to him that the Soviet system rules out, or at least considerably restricts those methods of keeping down the mass consumption which are practicable under a capitalist system. The widely accepted argument about the possibility of stepping-up the rate of saving (and consequently of investment) by the amount of luxury consumption by former capitalists and landlords failed to impress him. What was gained at the expense of upper-class consumption was largely absorbed by the high overhead cost of mushrooming bureaucratic apparatus, "an inevitable consequence of the low level of productive forces and of culture."[5] This did not imply any adverse judgment on the efficacy of planning as such. On the contrary, Bazarov was firmly convinced that a planned economy, even when operating under the not very propitious circumstances of a backward country, could demonstrate its superiority over capitalism, other things being equal, and, more particularly, permit "a more rational utilization of that part of the national income which is spent for reconstruction." * The actual hitch consisted in the fact that "other things" need not be equal: the amount of resources which could be released from current consumption under the conditions of the Soviet economy of the middle 'twenties was bound to be smaller than in prewar Russia.

◻

In brief, the two components of the familiar dilemma made their appearance once again. On the other hand, the capital requirements for reconstruction loomed large both in terms of the volume of investment per unit of time and of the length of the gestation period. On the other, voluntary or enforceable savings clearly were insufficient to secure the unfolding of the investment process without inflationary disturbances. But while Bazarov's diagnosis was practically identical with that of the leftists and of the moderates, his conclusions were different. As against the Left, he held that "in the spheres where the development of productive forces requires a considerable increase in fixed capital we are unable to maintain a high tempo of reconstruction." [6] Equally significant was his refusal to commit himself "every day and every hour" to what he termed "directive inequalities" such as a higher tempo of economic growth in the USSR than in capitalist countries, a larger increase in the output of producers goods than of consumers goods, faster expansion in industry than in agriculture.[7]

But at the same time he stressed again and again the decisive importance of the "problem of tempo" [8] and firmly rejected the idea of side-tracking heavy industries for some

---

* "O metodologii postroeniya perspektivnykh planov," *PKh* (July 1926), p. 11. In an article, written two years later, Bazarov put particular stress on the ability of the Soviet system to achieve a higher degree of capacity utilization than is possible under capitalism. This explained, in his view, the fact that the Soviet industrial production continued to grow at a fairly high rate also after having passed the prewar level. ("O perspektivakh khozyaistvennogo i kul'turnogo razvitiya," *EO* [June 1928], pp. 61–62.)

time to come. In his reply to Shanin's 1925 article he argued that the general postponement of investments in heavy industry would be definitely detrimental also to the objectives of those who advanced such a proposal. The increase in the volume of trade between city and village would require an expansion of railroad and river transportation facilities — and this would require a large volume of heavy industrial goods. In the interests of foreign trade it would be necessary to promote not only agriculture but also a number of capital-consuming extractive industries with favorable export possibilities. In other words, it was impossible to make headway even in the directions advocated by Shanin without an expansion of some lines of the heavy industries at home. Moreover, where the industries in question did not have to be created from scratch but were already in existence, the failure to allot certain minimum amounts of capital to them would imply not only a sacrifice of the potential gain, but also an actual decline from the present level:

It must be remembered that for a growing organism an interruption in development implies not a stationary condition but a step backward. . . . If we had neglected for several years the metallurgy and the metal-working trades, then, at the moment when according to this [Shanin's] plan it would be timely to develop these industries, they would be already worn out, debilitated, and run down to such an extent that there would be nothing left to develop but it would be necessary to start afresh. To embark upon such an experiment would mean to risk a loss not merely of building and equipment, but also of a productive force which is still a great deal more valuable and difficult to replace — the cadres of skilled metal workers.[9]

The notion of developing agriculture ahead of industry was, in his view, no less self-defeating. Such a policy would involve a shift in the terms of trade against agriculture (or, in the best case, a perpetuation of the present far-from-favorable "scissors" relationship). Yet the peasants were no longer in the mood to accept such a state of affairs because their demand for industrial goods was now more price-elastic than before:

As long as the satisfaction of most urgent and irreplaceable needs in industrial goods is involved, the peasant sells the surplus of his production on terms which are clearly unfavorable for him. Yet it does not follow therefrom that he will strive, under the prevailing value relationships, to expand his consumption of the industrial products beyond the level of the absolutely indispensable, and to raise correspondingly his own marketable output. . . . In spite of abundant crops [due to the record harvest of 1925] . . . the peasant is not inclined . . . to throw upon the market at a lowered price new quantities of the available surplus in order to elicit from the city, at raised price, new quantities of [industrial] commodities.[10]

All this, no doubt, made the planner's task even more complex. The rejection of the meat-axe technique called for subtler devices of cutting the coat according to the cloth; and it was in this field that Bazarov made his most significant contribution.

◻

The one possibility of taking some of the edge off of the dilemma was hinted at in the very paragraph which contained the most concise exposition of the "theory of the levelling-off curve." After pointing out the discontinuity involved in the transition from "restoration" to a large-scale investment, Bazarov argued that the sharpness of this discontinuity is largely dependent on the use to which the investable resources are put, more concretely, whether they are used primarily for new construction or for renovation and partial revamping of the existing plant. He admitted readily that from the long-run point of view, "the obsolete plants should merely be kept going until the end of their service-life and would not warrant considerable investments since a small increase in the volume and even smaller rise in the level of the productive forces would be bought here at the high price of relatively very great outlays." But —

We clearly cannot avoid such "irrational" outlays. Indeed if we had decided to make only such investments which appear to be rational from the standpoint of the general plan [i.e., in the long run], we would have to channel the whole investable accumulation into new construction while restricting the outlays for keeping existing enterprises in operation to the limits of the current maintenance. As a result, we would get for the next period, while the new plants are still in process of construction, not merely a decline in tempo of growth but a complete constancy of output and a fall in the average productivity of industrial labor accompanied by a sharp rise in the wage-bill due to the increase in the number of workers in construction trades.

The obvious conclusion was that "in order to soften the difficulties of the transitional period, it is necessary, alongside the new construction . . . to spend very considerable means for plants which are notoriously bad, solely for the sake of achieving an immediate, although a relatively moderate, increase in their productivity." [11]

The necessity to compromise between stability and speed of progress would therefore require, for the period of the next several years, a relatively high ratio of partial to total reconstruction of the industrial plant. As the new productive units gradually entered operation, this ratio could correspondingly decline.

The second line of attack consisted in giving the new construction an appropriate structure, direction, and sequence in time. The desperate scarcity of capital made it imperative (as Bazarov rather awkwardly put it) "to achieve the greatest possible effect . . . with a smallest possible expenditure for capital construction." [12] This did not imply that the resulting increase in current output would be spurious or bought at the price of technological stagnation. Considerable advance was still possible. To begin with, in a backward country like Russia there was a big backlog of technological improvements which could be applied at a small cost, simply by way of disseminating knowledge. Above all, however, two specific trends in the contemporary technological development "could, if competently and systematically utilized, permit us to give our industrialization an exceptionally powerful sweep and to exceed greatly the tempo of growth of the capitalist countries in the corresponding period of their development." [13] The first covered all kinds of changes in the layout of plants and in the coordination of the particular elements of the productive process ("speeding up the work of mechanisms, accompanied by specialization and automatization of complex operations") which were at that time coming in clusters in European industry and which were bracketed under the catchword "rationalization." Another great opportunity lay in electrification, which made possible the use of nonorganic power without large-scale indivisible installations in the power-consuming units. Moreover, the possibility of transmitting the new kind of energy over wide distances at low cost would diminish the need for a concentration of production in the big cities and thus permit cutting down on one of the most formidable items of social overhead. Wide possibilities for raising the productivity of the millions employed in artisan and peasant production were provided thereby. The basic effect of all these developments was the same. Large increases in output were forthcoming without anything like a proportional increase in capital stock.

All these proposals, superficially, had one fundamental flaw in common: they seemed to ignore the fact that while the proposed policies might be capital-saving in their operation stage, they would be definitely capital-consuming in their construction stage. Bazarov was not unprepared for such objections. The reequipment of the economy, he argued, had to be taken up not in an all-around fashion but according to a definite sequence in time. "The rationalization in its most effective form can be fulfilled only under the conditions of a tremendously large production. That's why the possibility of mass production is the basic criterion for determining the sequence of our reconstruction activities." The first priority should go to "lines which produce mass-consumption goods and those types of means of production the demand for which has already reached sufficiently large proportions." The other industries should not be reequipped for the time being. Their outputs could be supplemented out of imports and "concessions" to the foreign capital. An attempt to disregard this time-sequence and to press forward the expansion all along the line would have most calamitous effects.

Our lack of organizational and technological preparedness and the irrational diffusion of resources which such a superficial industrial expansion must inevitably imply will mean that the new plants, after having absorbed, in their sum total, huge capital outlays, will be condemned to a miserable vegetation, suffering endless infantile diseases and throwing on the market negligible amounts of goods of very high unit cost and very low quality.[14]

The defense considerations would not permit applying the correct policy in an uncompromising fashion; but the resulting deviations from the "optimum" would be limited in scope:

In order to increase our defense capability, we are forced to establish and to develop enterprises which do not satisfy this principle [of rational time sequence]. But exceptions of this kind should be confined to the output of special purposes, to the group of *cadre* enterprises. With regard to all those areas of industrialization which are supposed to serve the "civilian" needs in peacetime, considerations of defense capability and considerations of the national economy as a whole coincide: the strengthening and increase of the economic power of the USSR is at the same time the strengthening of its defense capability.[15]

As was shown before, Bazarov by no means ignored the importance of small but quick increases in output. His position on the relative importance of new construction and the reconditioning of the old plant indicated this very clearly. But he was unwilling to push the policy of trading productivity for speed to the point of undertaking full-scale construction of the inferior kind of plant — an operation which would obviously commit larger resources, and tie them up for a longer period of time than in the case of "mending and making do." The sacrifice in the long-term productivity involved in such procedure was in his opinion far too high:

The specialization of production is not feasible, as long as its scale is limited. Consequently . . . we would be forced to invest a good deal in technological installation of an obsolete type — in installations the efficiency of which is much less than that of their Western European or American competitors. As a result, we would, when the conditions for mass-scale production were fulfilled, face in many cases the following alternatives: either to use up to the limits of physical wear and tear the plants which were obsolete before their birth . . . or to scrap millions of "labor-days" embodied in the non-rational construction.*

* "Printsipy postroeniya perspektivnykh planov," *PKh* (February 1928), p. 49. The blanket refusal to "invest in technological equipment of an obsolete type" might seem too categorical if the term "obsolete type" is taken to refer to any equipment that does not reflect the last word in technological knowledge. Yet the cited injunction makes perfectly good sense with regard to equipment which entails higher costs per unit of output, over the relevant time period, than the newer one, given the relative factor prices that are expected to rule during this period (or, in extreme cases, given *any* set of relative factor prices). In the latter case, moreover, Bazarov's misgivings about working obsolete plants to death or "scrapping millions of labor days" that went into them, would be fully justified. Allowing a machine to operate at a loss after a new invention had rendered it prematurely obsolete, or abandoning it if the prime costs at which it had been producing came to exceed the total unit costs involved in the use of a newer type, would be an inevitable price to be paid for technological progress. Investing in a machine known to be economically inferior even before it started to earn its "returns over cost," would represent plain and unadulterated waste. Bazarov was not explicit about these considerations which were less familiar to his audience than to Western economists; but they are clearly in keeping with the general line of his argument.

The situation was essentially the same with regard to electrification. Bazarov fully recognized that the maximization of the return to capital in the short run would not be an appropriate guide for investment policy in this particular sphere, nor in the analytically similar cases of transportation:

If the scale of the expansion of plants producing the means of production is determined by the actually revealed real needs, the power installations and construction of transportation lines should be geared not to the actual but to the potential demand. . . . When we are starting to construct a railroad network in some regions, we do not yet have the freight streams for which the network capacity is ultimately planned. We have already on hand, however, the material and human elements of production which are bound to remain disjointed and paralyzed because of the lack of roads and which will be, after construction of roads, drawn together into a productive operation whose output will saturate the newly-created transportation arteries.[16]

This statement could be interpreted as a standard description of "external economies" which would stimulate development in the area of their application and hereby bring about their own validation in the long run as their returns would eventually rise as a result of this development. Bazarov was clearly aware of the major implications of this "building ahead of demand." Although he did not spell them out in detail,* yet he was cautious in drawing practical conclusions. For the time being, he felt, the top priority in electrification should go to regions in which the density of population and development of industry had already reached a relatively high level, rather than to the areas which were yet to be opened up. "We must show particular circumspection with regard to those power installations which will be

---

* He might have pointed out that this rise can be viewed as a self-generating process started by the initial introduction of the project in question and operating partly through the multiplier effect (increase in real income) and partly through the complementarity relationship with industries whose construction was induced by the creation of the project and, when completed, allowed to use it to full capacity. As far as this latter point is concerned, the whole impression of the upward spiral is due to the fact that the different parts of an integrated setup are created not simultaneously but successively.

able to make full use of their capacity only after new industries requiring large capital outlays and long construction periods are created in regions serviced by them." [17] The drastic shortage of investable resources combined with desperate need for quick increase in output called here for self-restraint also.

The economy of capital in the process of expansion was indispensable not only in order to reduce the inflationary pressure and to prevent the capital resources from waste through overextension. It was equally important as a means for dealing with another weak spot of the Soviet economy — the problem of surplus population. The source of mass unemployment lay, in Bazarov's view, not in the deficiency of the aggregate demand, but in the shortage of capital. In this diagnosis he was, once more, close to Preobrazhenski and he was equally concerned about the labor-displacing effects of the technological progress. ("What will happen in the full swing of reconstruction when the cheap industrial output floods the countryside, releasing the labor-time of millions of men?")[18] The therapy he suggested was altogether different, however. The bulk of the rural unemployed should not move to the cities but should be absorbed either by agriculture itself or by "those lines of industry which can be combined with agriculture." [19] Another important outlet could be found in projects belonging to the nonagricultural sphere but similarly characterized by a low amount of capital per head. The "earth-moving works preliminary to road building and to setting up of hydroelectric installations" ranked particularly high in this connection. It was a happy coincidence indeed that both spheres, which were of crucial significance for the enlargement of productive capacity in an underdeveloped economy, could be easily operated on the basis of a labor-intensive technology.

But while Bazarov insisted upon greater efforts toward economizing scarce capital resources, he took strong exception to the view that labor-absorption considerations should be given precedence over efficiency. According to him, there were two extreme alternatives: (1) "With investment assumed equal, the labor-intensive alternative yields, as compared with the less labor-intensive one, an increase in the physical volume of output in proportion (or better than in proportion) to the increase in number of workers employed"; and (2) "With investment assumed equal, the more labor-intensive plant yields less output per employed worker than the less labor-absorbing plant." Bazarov strongly endorsed the application of labor-intensity criterion in the first case, and rejected it just as emphatically in the second:

It is sometimes maintained that it is worthwhile to make large investments in repair and reconditioning of technologically backward plants rather than to construct plants of a modern type which would allegedly threaten the proletariat with the increase of unemployment, as a result of excessive increase in productivity of labor. It is impossible to agree with such a position. The conservation of the backward technology for many years by large outlays for its reproduction in an unchanged, or almost unchanged, form is an outright negation of the planned reconstruction, a clear *testimonium paupertatis* of the principle of planning.*

It is not difficult to understand why Bazarov's pronouncements commanded attention and abiding respect even among those who disagreed with him in substance. Undoubtedly he had a clear vision of the problems to be solved and of the

* *PKh* (February 1928), pp. 52–53. The reader may notice that the attitude, so categorically condemned in the quoted paragraph, would in some instances coincide with the "mending-and-making-do" policy advocated by Bazarov in his earlier article and motivated by the desire to keep up the output flow per unit of capital high even at the price of a higher cost per unit of product. Hence, an economy obeying Bazarov's injunctions as to the inevitability of "irrational outlays" would occasionally be acting *as if* it were putting employment considerations first; but the difference in guiding considerations would prove relevant whenever the more labor-intensive alternative would *not* involve a larger increase in output.

conflicting considerations to be taken into account; and while his attempts to set forth clearcut criteria which would provide guidance in individual cases were, as will be shown later, less than fully successful, the broad lines of economic policy laid down by him were not affected by such errors. Bazarov had, moreover, an acute understanding of the economic techniques and institutional arrangements required for the successful execution of the policies he recommended. His discussion of these aspects of the situation revealed with striking clarity the basic "metaeconomic" attitudes underlying his whole conception.

Bazarov was, undoubtedly, an avowed advocate of a state-controlled economy. In his writings of an earlier period he had argued that "the period of imperialist and civil war produced such tremendous deformations in the system of our national economy and created such disproportions between parts that . . . a long-term rehabilitation program is needed." [20] He was equally emphatic concerning the need for centralized planning in the later years when he participated in preparing the initial drafts of the First Five Year Plan. The different orders of priorities he spoke about were to be set by the planning organs, and not left to the discretion of the "invisible hand." But the concentration of the basic investment decisions at the top did not preclude, in his view, the extensive use of market mechanism which alone

. . . makes it possible, under present circumstances, to provide an automatic check of the correctness of all actions [and acts like] an automatic calculating machine showing the results of the activities of each branch of the economy, and of each separate enterprise. I firmly believe that . . . the existence of market and economic accounting ("khozraschet") is the necessary prerequisite of any possible planning, whether there will be a world revolution or not.[21]

Several years later, in an article discussing the first draft of the Five Year Plan, he suggested that the introduction of a rate of interest on loans given to enterprises would impel the managers to treat time as a cost factor. The speed of the construction of new plants which was, in his view, one of the weakest spots of the Soviet economy would be greatly increased as a result:

> The concessionist counts as a loss every day during which his capital, invested in new construction, does not function productively, while it makes little difference to a [state] trust, as long as it builds not for the borrowed money but out of its "own" or out of a grant, whether or not the capital will lay idle for one year, two years, or several years. The state must collect from every ruble granted to industry a certain interest charge, which would not be too high but which should still make itself felt.[22]

It is easy to notice similarities between Bazarov's treatment of the function of the price mechanism and the position of Bukharin; and it is equally evident that ideas of both men, rudimentary as they are, have a good deal in common with the recent conceptions of the socialist economists in the West. They could be conveniently placed somewhere in the middle between the adherents of "democratic planning" and protagonists of pure "market socialism." The Soviet theorists, however, were more emphatic than some of their Western opposite numbers in linking up the discussion of techniques of economic administration with observations on the general climate and institutional setting in which these devices were to operate; and here Bazarov went several steps beyond Bukharin. He kept insisting, again and again, that age-old cultural backwardness coupled with the weakness of spontaneous and socially responsible individual action was the strongest obstacle to rapid economic growth in Russia. He fervently believed that this stumbling block could be removed only by creating conditions in which intellectual daring and the desire for change could freely assert themselves: the prime task of wise leadership should consist "in locating and cultivating carefully the spirit of creative initiative in individuals as well as in groups and in adapting to this basic objective all social 'superstructures.' " [23] He left no doubt as to his notions about the political aspects of these "superstructures" when he recalled, in one of his last recorded pronouncements, the dictum of the representatives of prerevolutionary gentry liberalism: "A constitution is indispensable even for the purpose of the construction of good maternity wards." [24] It was this notion of the ultimate identity between efficiency and freedom that underlay his thinking and was the basic reason for the incompatibility between his views and the increasingly important aspects of the situation he was confronted with. It was the refusal to renounce these views that doomed him later. But in the years under consideration the gulf seemed less impassable than it eventually turned out to be. And while the distinguished "honest nonparty man," as Bazarov half-jokingly referred to himself, remained on the side lines of the battle royal raging within the Bolshevik ranks, the ideas expounded by him were closely approximated in the new attitude of the faction which at that time was responsible for Soviet economic policy.

NOTE

For the sake of chronological correctness it should be noted that it was Vladimir G. Groman, Bazarov's close friend and one of the outstanding Soviet statisticians, who offered the first version of the theory of "levelling-off curve" in an article published in early 1925. The debacle of the Civil War, he stressed, affected different spheres of the economy to a different extent. Agriculture, due to the "primitiveness of the process of production, direct connection of the existence of the people with the results of this production (and) indestructibility of the main means of production, the land" showed a relatively small decline in output while industry "consisting of complex productive agglomerations was bound to lose its capacity to produce as a result of spoilage, destruction, and temporary lack even of a few elements." In the process of recovery this basic difference in technology worked in favor of industry. Although in the midtwenties industrial output did not yet come as close to its prewar level as agricultural output did, industry approached this benchmark more rapidly than agriculture because in the former "the restoration of a small amount of missing components has set into motion a huge volume of productive forces." [25]

This was, no doubt, a simplified but basically correct description of that phase of Soviet economic recovery in which "easy expansion" was still gaining momentum. But Groman weakened his position by a piece of statistical eccentricity. He claimed to have established that the ratio between the values of marketable industrial and agricultural output in the second and third years of the recovery came very close to the 63/37 ratio which had expressed, according to his estimates, the ratio between the values of outputs of these two spheres in 1913. Groman interpreted this as an indication (1) that the changes in relative prices since the prewar period tend to offset almost exactly the changes in relative levels of output, and (2) that the steady increase in industrial supplies followed by a continual decline in unit costs due to an improving capacity utilization would close the "scissors" and bring not only the total output values but also the relative prices of agricultural and industrial goods back to the prewar level. He was emphatic in stressing that the constancy of this ratio would hold only as long as economic recovery was confined to the full utilization of capacity in its size and structure inherited from the prewar period:

We are obviously and evidently approaching the prewar ratio of the relative sizes of agriculture and industry. But whether we shall reach it or even go beyond it, will depend on the way in which we will solve the problem of fixed capital. . . . The relationship of the [agricultural and industrial] price levels . . . will go beyond the prewar norm . . . if we industrialize the country and carry out at the same time a technological reconstruction which will reduce the [industrial] unit costs.[26]

These qualifications are undoubtedly sufficient to show the dishonesty of the streamlined official economists in later years who tried to interpret Groman's statements about the 63/37 ratio as a sinister attempt to freeze forever the relationship between Soviet industry and agriculture at the level of backward Tsarist Russia. But after obviously fraudulent criticisms are discarded, the idea that the movements of the prices of agricultural and industrial goods exactly compensate the opposite movements in the respective outputs, still remains astounding. It involves assumptions about the immutability of demand and inflexibility of supply over the whole intervening period which are truly breathtaking even when explicitly restricted to the years before resumption of large-scale investment activity. It was not surprising, therefore, that while Groman's presentation of the general characteristics of Soviet recovery was widely accepted and elaborated upon, his attempts to forecast were an easy target for attacks.

IV
The Bukharin School Readjusts
Its Views

THE first reaction of Bukharin and his followers to the new problems was the refusal to recognize their existence. In a polemic against Georgi L. Pyatakov, a leader of the left-wing opposition, who was the first to submit the problem of the arrears in replacement to public debate,[1] Bukharin chided his opponent for the failure to appreciate the full impact of the increase in the speed of turnover of capital. After stressing triumphantly that Pyatakov had been forced to recognize economies in working capital resulting from an increase in this speed, Bukharin concluded: "All this, of course, has a very close relation also to the problem of the reproduction of fixed capital." [2] The fact that the latter task required larger and more protracted investment effort than the first did not seem worth mentioning. But a statement made later in the course of the same year seemed to indicate a change in mood. "We have come to the conclusion that we can build socialism even on this wretched technological level . . . that we shall move at a snail's pace, but that we shall be building socialism and that we shall build it." [3] This declaration became almost immediately the favorite target of attacks from the left, and very logically so. It was certainly part and parcel of the political philosophy which had produced the ill-fated "get-rich" slogan. But in terms of economic policy, it represented a new variation — the acquiescence in the "snail's pace" sounded considerably less sanguine than earlier promises of the "very quick tempo of growth."

Out of these ambiguities a modified line of policy gradually emerged. Basic elements of the old approach were, no doubt, still in evidence; indeed, they were stressed as emphatically as ever. "Our economy," Bukharin declared, "exists for the consumer, and not the consumer for the economy." He praised this "new economy" which "differs from the old by taking as its guiding principle the needs of the masses and not the profit you are earning on Monday and Tuesday without thinking of what will happen on Thursday and Friday"; and he felt certain that the policy of keeping industrial prices down would force the plant managers to lower costs.[4] At the same time, however, a new note crept into his pronouncements. He recognized that the Soviet economy was now facing a transition from the "period of restoration" to the "period of reconstruction." This assignment whose fulfillment "depends primarily upon our success in acquiring and applying capital . . . for the expansion of the basis of production, for the construction or the laying down of the new enterprises, to a considerable extent on a new technical basis" constituted "the task of greatest difficulty."[5] Aleksei I. Rykov, Lenin's successor as chairman of the Council of People's Commissars and Bukharin's *alter ego* in matters of economic and general policy, was even more explicit and specific:

The country can no longer live without capital investments. The present high prices of industrial goods are in many respects due, of course, to inadequate economic organization, high overhead costs, and so on. But the main and enduring cause of these high prices is the wornout condition of our industrial equipment. . . . Full utilization of acreage formerly belonging to big private owners [and] exhaustion of land-intensive methods of agriculture make it impossible for the peasants, particularly in densely settled regions, to extend their economy on the basis of its backward technology.[6]

He restated this position even more pointedly in a rebuttal to Sokol'nikov several months later:

> The crucial problem consists now not in securing the satisfaction of "the most simple, elementary and primitive needs," as Comrade Sokol'nikov says. This is already a past stage. . . . Comrade Sokol'nikov considers "the improvement in technology, the increase in fixed capital of the country" a task of the future. Actually, however, these tasks are facing us squarely at present.[7]

The new strategy in polemics reflected this change in attitude. There was no longer any attempt at sidestepping the harsh problems. The emphasis was, indeed, on the need for prudence in dealing with them. A telling point was scored, as we have already seen,[8] by turning against the left-wing opposition one of its chief weapons. The goods famine, it was argued, would be aggravated and not relieved by channeling resources into time-consuming investment processes on the scale suggested by Preobrazhenski and his friends. The tensions generated by such a policy would threaten to undo the achievements of the NEP period. At this point another shift in the argument became apparent. Not the deficiency of peasant demand but its excess over the available supply of industrial goods was now recognized as the main danger, and the dreadful retaliation weapon of the peasantry against the price increases of industrial products was seen no longer in the peasant buyers' strike but in the reduction of their supplies which would play havoc with the operations of industry. Moreover, the price increase would hit with particular severity the poor peasants, deepen therewith the social polarization of the peasantry which the Left had been so alarmed about, and intensify the exodus from the villages to the cities, thus aggravating the problem of unemployment still further.[9]

The impact of the "leftist" policy on the relationship between city and village was the main theme of the Bukharin group. This was, however, not the only source of danger. The critique of their ambitious industrialization plans was bolstered by reference to the distortions which they were bound to cause within the nonagricultural field as well. The scarecrow of "Tuganism" was no longer brought in; not the lack of investment outlets but the various manifestations of capital shortage appeared now to be the critical problem. The tendency to sink all available resources in the construction of new equipment, Rykov stressed, would mean that newly-built plants would, owing to the lag in raw material supplies, remain partly idle for a time; the evident waste of resources resulting therefrom would be accentuated by the possibility that the plants in question would become prematurely obsolete because of the delay in the start of their operation.[10] Another source of potential disturbance lay in the impact of sudden changes on an economy operating under a severe strain: "We do not always have sufficient reserves when it is necessary to make some considerable unforeseen expenditures in order to fill this or that hole on some segment of the economic front."[11]

Bukharin spoke in a similar vein: "We cannot maneuver with those resources which already exist and, after having invested a definite amount in capital construction, we cannot reallocate it in a different way. We are extremely constrained."[12] While pressing forward "the rationalization as well as the renewal and expansion of fixed capital" it was imperative to abandon erroneous notions about the relative shares of investment-goods industries and consumers-goods industries in the planned expansion.

We believe that the formula which calls for a maximum of investments in heavy industry is not quite correct, or rather, quite incorrect. If we have to put the main emphasis on the development of the means of production, we must combine this development with a corresponding expansion of light industry which has a quicker turnover and repays within a shorter time the amounts spent on it. We must attempt to get the optimal combination of both.*

And in the same speech he pointed out that the policy of spreading the limited resources thin by distributing them over a large number of simultaneously started constructional projects would result in a greater delay in completion of each of them and, consequently, in a longer average gestation period of the aggregate investment in question than if the same amounts had been concentrated on a smaller front.

A more complete treatment of these problems was given in "Zametki ekonomista" which was Bukharin's last major published pronouncement on economic policy.[13] In this article Bukharin summed up his views on the nature of Soviet industrialization. He emphasized once more that "the greatest sustained speed is achieved when industry develops on the basis provided by the rapidly growing agriculture." At the same time he brought out very clearly the point which had been conspicuous by its absence in his writings of the earlier period: "In a semipauper country we must raise enormous sums of fresh 'capital' and apply them productively by converting them into new technology, new buildings, etc." The crux of the article, however, consisted not in an exposition of these general ideas but in an analysis of the actual situation of the Soviet economy. After noting that "industry itself . . . which is developing at record speed develops at the same time a record demand for industrial

---

* "Ob itogakh ob'edinennogo plenuma TsK and TsKK VKP(b)," *P*, November 4, 1927. It is evident (although Bukharin did not make it explicit) that the meaning of the term "quicker turnover" underwent a change. Up to now it was used to emphasize increases in output due to a more intensive utilization of existing plant, while in the present context it is mentioned in connection with "optimal combination" between different time patterns of full-scale investment in *new* plants. The criteria for determining the "optimal combination" are not explained—a fairly typical case in the debate in which the concept of optimum was bandied around quite freely but not defined.

goods and is not able to satisfy it," Bukharin went on to specify the key bottlenecks in which these limitations would become manifest ("not quite correct proportions between the different branches of industry, with metallurgy, to take an example, lagging behind considerably"; "not quite correct proportions between the growth of the current production of industry and the growth of capital investment"; shortage of vital raw materials of agricultural origin). As a result, "the overextension of the capital expenditure (1) will not be paralleled by the actual constructive activity of a corresponding size; (2) will inevitably cause after a lapse of some time an interruption of the projects already started; (3) will exert, in many directions, [unfavorable] effects on other lines of production; (4) will aggravate the goods famine all around; (5) will eventually retard the tempo of development." It was in this context that Bukharin coined the phrase which later became famous — "even according to Boehm-Bawerk, it is impossible to build a present-day factory with future bricks." The marked increase in incisiveness and power of analysis as compared with earlier pronouncements reflected, no doubt, the actual developments in the Soviet economy; and these developments had already moved, as we shall see later, beyond the limits of what Bukharin and his political friends considered safe and sound.

◙

The battle lines against the extremists on the Right and Left were clearly drawn herewith. The representatives of the Bukharin-Rykov group, while admitting the necessity of "huge capital outlays" emphasized the need to keep the over-all rate of expansion within certain limits. They were equally categorical in their refusal to assign to any section of the economy a degree of preponderance which would involve a temporary halt or actual retrogression of the others. These basic principles were backed up by an argument which resembled very much that of Bazarov and which purported to prove that considerable room for maneuver was still left. A good deal of significance was attached to the fact that the relative advantages of more capital-using compared to less capital-using methods varied in importance as between different lines of production. "The tractor," Bukharin stressed, "is applicable [only] in the cultivation of grain, in the first place — in the sphere of extensive farming"; [14] and Rykov seconded him by pointing out that "the possibilities of increase in yields even by such relatively elementary devices as replacing the wooden hoe by plough, improvements in seeds, introduction of the simplest agricultural machinery and of fertilizers are tremendous at the present level of our villages." [15] Another promising possibility consisted in the development of such kinds of agricultural production as animal breeding and gardening which are more labor intensive than grain cultivation. These policies were expected to score two hits at one blow. They would result in an expansion in output at moderate cost, and would go a long way toward absorbing the rural surplus population without requiring large capital outlays per head of the newly employed.

But even within the industrial sector, in spite of the generally pronounced superiority of "capitalistic" technology in this field and of the crying need for large replacement expenditures, every attempt was to be made to promote growth while keeping capital costs down. The resolutions of the Fifteenth Party Congress which met in December 1927, and whose policy declaration reflected in every respect the new attitude of the Bukharin group, provide an extensive catalogue of ways to economize capital as they were seen at that time. The small-scale manufacturing and the handicrafts which accounted for 35 per cent of the gross output of industrial consumers goods before the war[16] and which had been Lenin's great hope in the early years of the NEP were ex-

pected to "help alleviate the goods shortage and reduce unemployment";[17] in the process of this development, they
were to undergo a technological "rationalization" and to be
gradually transformed along the lines of producers' cooperation. Wherever large-scale industrial reconstruction and expansion could no longer be postponed, the unsettling potentialities of massive capital outlays were to be kept at bay
by an increase in the efficiency of the construction work, and
by greater care in investment planning. While acknowledg-
ing the need for increased emphasis on capital-goods' industries, the Fifteenth Congress called attention to the "danger
of an excessive tieup of capital in large construction which
will be realized on the market only after several years." *
It warned with equal bluntness against the "danger of tying
up unbearably large means on too broad a front of capital
construction, given the impossibility of realizing them [on
the market] without a long delay." Instead, "maximal effectiveness of the investment both as to the completion time
of the projects and the productive effect of plants under
construction" was demanded.[18] Last but not least, the opportunities of cheap expansion in the early NEP style could
get a new lease on life. The reduction of working hours
would permit the introduction of the multiple-shift system
on a large scale and thus extend the possibilities for an
increase in utilization of the existing capacity — another development which would have favorable effects on output
and employment.

All these policies, whose common purpose was to compress

* VKP, XV s'ezd, p. 1293. A much more dubious proposition is contained
in the next sentence: "On the other hand, it should be remembered that
the quicker turnover in light industry permits the utilization of its capital
also for construction in the heavy industry under the condition of development of light industry." At best, this is based on confusion of micro- and
macroeconomic approaches — an error which, as will be seen later, was
fatal also for the much more ingenious argument of Shanin. Less charitably,
the reasoning comes perilously close to an attempt to eat cake and have
it, too.

the capital requirements of the planned expansion, had to be paralleled by attempts to raise the rate of savings. A shift from the position of 1925 was evident here, too. The time was thought to be ripe for a stiffened policy toward the upper stratum of the peasantry: "We are now in a position to exert a stronger pressure upon our main adversary, the kulaks.[19] If there is a possibility to take more from the top stratum, we should do it. During the last two years we have increased the [tax] progression enormously." [20]

This change in attitude toward the village rich, it was stressed, was made possible by the rise in the general level of agriculture, accompanied by a strengthening of the bonds between the Soviet regime and the main body of the peasantry — a development which would be unthinkable if the recommendations of the left-wing opposition had been followed. Yet Bukharin and his associates continued to pin high hopes on voluntary saving which was to be attracted "through loans of all possible kinds, through saving banks, etc." [21] In order to promote such savings, however, it was imperative to remove uncertainties and fears which were haunting the potential savers: "Why does the peasant not want to wait with the money [he obtained in fall for the sale of his products], say, a few months, but parts with it immediately? Because our money is not yet stable enough to serve for accumulation purposes." The sharp practices of some local governmental agencies which were willing to supply industrial goods only in barter against grain and which forced the peasants to sign up for state loans were cited as another cause for the unwillingness to save.[22] Also with regard to the hoards of grain a cautious approach was advocated. These hoards, Rykov argued in early 1927, were created not so much for the purpose of profiteering as in order to build up reserves against possible droughts.[23] But also in 1928 when the hoarding assumed (for reasons to be discussed later) much more serious dimensions, he was emphatic in warning that reliance on forcible seizure in attempts to reduce the hoards would revive memories of War Communism and cause a violent reaction not only on the part of kulak but of the bulk of the "middle peasantry" as well.[24]

□

Such were, in broad outline, the main levers the Bukharin-Rykov group intended to rely on in its attempts to close the "inflationary gap" of the reconstruction period. The new position of this group clearly represented a significant departure from the earlier views of its leading theorist; and there was certainly a broad consistency between the diagnosis and the prescriptions. True, the reasoning was still showing a tendency to slip over some complexities which were fairly apparent even on a purely analytical level and which were bound to make the going rougher than the argumentation of the leading advocates of the policy in question might lead their audience to believe. There was no attempt to face the uncomfortable fact that a steep increase in the progressiveness of taxation and the stimulation of voluntary saving could be reconciled only by some deliberate policies, and that the plain income tax was not necessarily the most promising method toward that purpose. The repeated references to "rationalization" and its cost-reducing effects failed to allow for the fact that these improvements had an impressive initial cost of their own — a point which, as we saw, had been clearly recognized by Bazarov. The high expectations roused by the prospective increase in the number of shifts, finally, were not tempered by the recognition that the rise in the intensity of the utilization of the overaged plant would speed up the physical deterioration of existing equipment and consequently increase the need for replacement, thus reducing the net gain secured.*

It is unlikely that Bukharin and Rykov were ignorant of these and similar points of detail. But in spite of their failure to enter the necessary caveats, they were not complacent in arguing their case. They were, no doubt, firmly convinced that the "American way" of combining a high rate of investment with a steady rise of the consumption levels of the urban and agricultural population could be emulated under the very different conditions of the Soviet economy of the twenties. The sum total of the policies outlined above, they felt, would be instrumental in bringing this about. But while the resolutions of the Fifteenth Congress spoke in ringing tones of confidence, their spiritual godfathers did not attempt to hide that the situation was bound to be touch and go for quite a while. True, they continued to insist that "we cannot and we must not choose the path of development at which the tasks of keeping up the highest possible tempo and of maintaining the moving equilibrium of the whole economic system exclude each other." But the significance of this statement was considerably reduced by the frank admission that "there is no guaranty" against "temporary imbalance" as long as there are no adequate reserves of raw materials, foodstuffs, finished goods, gold, etc.[25] The building-up of such safety margins would

---

* A curious attempt at converting this limitation into a source of strength was made two years later by V. Motylev, a noted Soviet economist. After stating that "the increase in the number of shifts and continuous production will intensify the wear and tear of the equipment and will shorten its service life, particularly in the old enterprises," he goes on to conclude: "The amortization allowances will grow, and this will permit the increase of capital outlays," and "replacement of the worn-out and obsolete equipment by the new and more efficient will be speeded up" (*Problema tempa razvitiya SSSR* [3 ed., Moscow, 1929], p. 124). As if the growth of amortization had automatically guaranteed the possibility of extended replacement activity — and as if the crucial problem had consisted in lack of incentive to introduce "new and more efficient equipment" rather than in the shortage of capital!

be possible only by slowing down the tempo of capital construction — a policy which was now ruled out. It was therefore only logical for Rykov to declare that "if we want to develop heavy industry out of our own resources, and we must do it, we will have to retrench ourselves somewhat for a time." [26] The "temporary excesses of demand over supply" were now accepted as well-nigh inevitable. The crucial task was to prevent them from reaching a level of "general economic crisis." The leaders of the Trotskyite opposition would find here little to disagree with. True, the left-wingers were still setting the "tempos" higher and were ready to rely in the main on the drastic levies imposed on the peasantry while the Bukharin-Rykov group preferred the methods of "repressed inflation." But these differences, important as they were, could not alter the fundamental fact that the former "harmonists" and the proponents of "primitive socialist accumulation" were by now solidly on the horns of the same dilemma, and none of them found this a comfortable position.

V

An Exercise in Evasion

FOLLOWING a survey of the contributions of the leading participants to the debate, an account of Stalin's views is apt to be anti-climactic, to put it mildly. Indeed, the pronouncements on controversial issues of economic policy which the Secretary-General was making up to the end of 1927 exhibit such a firm resolve to be against sin and to be in favor of eating one's cake and having it too, that it appears, at first, almost hopeless to distill out of them a clear view not only of the nature of the problems, but also of the attitude of the man. But after a close examination of the record, there can be no doubt that Stalin's statement at the Fourteenth Party Congress: "We are, and we shall be, for Bukharin," * provides a substantially correct description of his position at that time. True, in certain respects he sounded a somewhat different note. He showed a strong inclination, on every propitious occasion, to exalt the glories of the coming industrialization. Moreover, the aspect of the future developments which received his fondest attention was the possibility of making Russia a self-contained unit, economically independent of the outside world — "a country which can produce by its own efforts the necessary equipment." [1] He started to emphasize the need for the intensive reconstruction of Soviet industry earlier than Bukharin did; and in the same speech in which he dramatically refused to give

* VKP, *XIV s'ezd*, p. 494. In the seventh volume of Stalin's collected works, where the text of this speech is given, the words "and we shall be" are omitted.

"Bukharin's blood" to the opposition, he did not hesitate to disassociate himself from the "get rich" slogan.[2] But neither these nor similar instances could alter the fact that on issues which were relevant for actual policy the agreement was practically complete. When Stalin was applauding the removal of "administrative obstacles preventing the rise in the peasant welfare" as "an operation [which] undoubtedly facilitates any accumulation, private capitalist as well as socialist,"[3] or when he denounced on an earlier occasion any attempt to fan the class struggle in the village as "empty chatter," while praising peasant cooperation as a road toward the socialist transformation of agriculture,[4] he was talking like a Bukharinite pure and simple. His wailings about "get rich" sounded, in view of this, very much like the famous admonition given to Eduard Bernstein, the father of German Social Democratic "revisionism," by one of his senior friends: "Such things should be done but not said." The identity of views on the larger issue of relationships between industry and agriculture was equally evident. Although Stalin did not invoke the ghost of Tugan-Baranovski (he was at that time somewhat chary of incursions into the field of theory), he believed firmly that "our industry, which provides the foundation of socialism and of our power, is based on the internal, on the peasant market."[5]

The last point, on the face of it, did not jibe very well with his other declared objectives. If industry had to be oriented primarily toward the satisfaction of peasant needs, it would be impossible to spare an adequate amount of resources for a large-scale effort toward the reconstruction of industry, particularly if this should be done with an eye to future self-sufficiency in the sphere of capital-goods production. But to proclaim long-term goals was one thing, and to rush toward them at a high speed was another. Stalin in these days showed no inclination of the latter kind. In the same speech in which he extolled the virtues of economic independence, he readily admitted that large-scale imports of machinery were, at least for the time being, indispensable for the development of the Soviet economy. At a somewhat later date he went to considerable lengths to emphasize, in polemics against Trotsky, that the Soviet Union would not endanger her economic sovereignty by trading extensively with the capitalist world; first of all, the dependence involved would be a two-way affair ("our country depends on other countries just as other countries depend on our national economy"), and secondly, nationalization of large-scale industry and banking as well as the state monopoly of foreign trade would provide effective safeguards against foreign encroachments.* The position with regard to the rate of industrial development was characterized by similar circumspection. At one point Stalin would attempt to sidetrack the issue by injecting a larger one and by insisting that a reconstruction of fixed capital in industry would not solve the problem of building socialism in Russia as long as agriculture had not been transformed along collectivist lines.[6] On another occasion, he praised glowingly the rapid increase in the output of the Soviet metal industry as proof that "the proletariat . . . can construct with its own efforts a new industry and a new society," [7] without mentioning the obvious fact that this increase had been so rapid precisely because it had been based on increased utilization of the old industrial capacity and *not* on the creation of the new. But when he had to face the problem squarely in his report to the Fourteenth Party Congress, he left no doubts as to his real attitude:

In order to switch from the maximal utilization of everything we had in industry to the policy of constructing a new industry on a new technological basis, on the basis of the construction of

* *Sochineniya*, IX, 132–133. In the same speech, incidentally, Stalin indulged (albeit not without Trotsky's active prodding) in one of the rare "self-criticisms" of his career. He admitted that in 1922 he had favored the relaxation of the foreign trade monopoly.

new plants, large capital outlays are needed. But since we are suffering considerable capital shortage, the further development of our industry will proceed, in all probability, not at such a fast rate as it has until now. The situation with regard to agriculture is different. It cannot be said that all potentialities of agriculture are already exhausted. Agriculture, as distinct from industry, can move for some time at a fast rate also on its present technological basis. Even the simple rise in the cultural level of the peasant, even such a simple thing as cleaning the seeds could raise the gross output of agriculture by 10 to 15 per cent . . . That's why the further development of agriculture does not yet face the technological obstacles that our industry has to face. . . .[8]

Stalin could not have been more frank in formulating the basic problem which was, as we have seen time and time again, at the core of the whole discussion. The very same factors — limited productive capacity and low levels of income — that called for expansion in Soviet industry were putting obstacles in its way. In the quoted paragraph the emphasis was clearly on the obstacles. Still, when Shanin applauded heartily,[9] he must have done so with a twinkle in his eye. In fact, the Fourteenth Party Congress signalized the transition from "filling-in" to reconstruction — but reconstruction on a limited scale and in a cautious mood. Although the volume of capital outlays increased substantially in the years 1926 and 1927, the leftists led by Preobrazhenski and Trotsky immediately opened fire. The new investment program, they claimed, was neither here nor there — too limited to secure an increase in capacity large enough to stabilize the situation in a not-too-distant future, yet too ambitious not to cause inflationary disturbances now in view of the absence of drastic taxation measures.

In the face of these attacks, and of actual difficulties which did not fail to materialize, something more than a sober and judicious description of the two horns of the dilemma was called for. A characteristic division of labor developed at this point. Bukharin and Rykov, the guiding spirits of the revised line, were wrestling with large, clearcut issues — the relation between heavy and light industry, the limits for investment in time-consuming projects, the possibility of absorbing the surplus labor in production lines with low capital requirements — in a desperate search for solutions which would make the adopted policy work. Stalin followed a different procedure. He visibly tried to avoid sharply delineated problems. Instead, he let his argument see-saw from bold statements of principles to sobering but comfortably loose observations on present-day realities, and he switched from obtuse mystique to gruff common sense. Rapid industrialization? Yes, indeed! More than that — it should be kept in mind that "not every development of industry constitutes industrialization" and that "the focal point of industrialization, its basis, consists of the development of heavy industry (fuel, metals, etc.) and of the eventual development of production of the means of production, development of domestic machine-building." [10] But right on the heels of such proclamations there would come a slap at those who "sometimes forget that it is impossible to make plans either for industry as a whole or for some 'large and all-embracing' enterprise without a certain minimum means, without a certain minimum of reserves," * and warning that "an industry which breaks itself away from the national economy as a whole

---

* *Sochineniya*, VIII, 131. It is not unlikely that the disparaging remark about "some 'large and all-embracing' enterprise" refers to the famous Dnieper Dam whose construction was under consideration at that time. According to Trotsky's note of April 14, 1927 (available at the Trotsky Archives of Houghton Library, Harvard University [no. 421C]), the minutes of the session of the Central Committee of the CPSU held in April 1926 contain (p. 110) the following passage from Stalin's speech: "It is a matter of building Dneprostroi out of our own means. And the means that are needed are large — several hundred millions. We should be careful not to get into position of that peasant who after having saved some extra money, instead of fixing his plough or improving his farm, bought a record player, and — went broke. Can we ignore resolutions of the Congress which say that our plans should be adapted to our resources?"

and loses its connection with it cannot be the guiding force of the national economy." [11] Could the Soviet economy in its present shape afford a rate of economic development which would exceed that of the capitalist countries? Of course! The capitalist countries had based their expansion on the exploitation of colonies, military conquest, or foreign loans. But the Soviet Union expropriated the capitalists and the landlords, nationalized strategic areas of the economy, and repudiated the Tsarist foreign debts. This circumstance enabled her to provide a sufficient volume of accumulation without having recourse to any of these devices.[12] Furthermore, it permitted this accumulation to unfold alongside of "a steady improvement in the material conditions of the working masses, including the bulk of the peasantry . . . as contrasted with the capitalist methods of industrialization based on the growing misery of millions of working people." [13] Specific reasons in support of these encouraging assertions were not given. However, the most elaborate of such homilies concluded by admitting that the socialist principles along which the Soviet economy was organized offered merely a possibility of achieving the appropriate level of accumulation, but no more than that. More important, the concrete proposals for policy which followed were in their sum total excruciatingly modest, not only in comparison with the grandiloquent claims that preceded them, but also with regard to the size of the investment programs they were supposed to sustain. They represented, in essence, a diluted and incomplete version of policies advocated by Bukharin and Rykov. The "authority of our credit institutions" had to be raised in order to encourage private savings; retail prices were to be reduced; industrial enterprises were to make provisions for amortization and further expansion; reserves of exportable grain were to be built up; budgetary surpluses were to be secured.[14] On other occasions elimination of waste and inefficiency in economic and political administration received the top billing.[15] Some of these measures, while pointing in the right direction, could hardly be expected to have much effect in the immediate future; others were of the pious-wish variety or involved putting the cart before the horse, as in the case of price reductions not preceded by substantial expansion in productive capacity.

All this looked very much like trying to buy a second-hand Ford for the price of a discarded piece of junk while pretending that a brand-new Cadillac was being obtained. True, there was another line of defense: to play down the importance of the recurrent spells of goods famine and to present them as transient phenomena. Although Stalin tried this device occasionally, it was obviously a tenuous argument to use, particularly since the assertion that "quick development of our industry is the surest way to eliminate the goods famine,"[16] sounded too much like conceding a point to the Left opposition. It was therefore only logical for him to shift the battleground to the territory of the adversaries, to concentrate on the crucial weak spot in their position and to pound relentlessly upon it:

The oppositionist bloc assumed a conflict between industry and agriculture and is headed toward breaking industry away from agriculture. It does not realize and it does not admit that it is impossible to develop industry while neglecting the interests of agriculture and hurting these interests in a rude fashion. It does not understand that if industry is the guiding force of the national economy, the agricultural economy represents in turn the basis on which our industry is able to develop . . . The Party cannot and will not tolerate [a situation in which] the opposition continues to undermine the basis of the alliance of workers and peasants by spreading the idea of an increase in wholesale prices and in the burden of taxation upon the peasantry, by attempting to "construe" the relationships between proletariat and peasantry not as relationships of economic *cooperation* but as relationships of exploitation of the peasantry by the proletarian state. The Party cannot and will not tolerate this.[17]

At the Fifteenth Party Congress, which met one year later and carried out this solemn vow by expelling the leftwingers, Stalin was surveying the field once more. His report displayed the full array of the familiar arguments: praise for the growth of the Soviet industrial output at a rate showing "a record percentage which no large capitalist country in the world has ever shown";[18] reaffirmation of faith in the superiority which the Soviet system had over capitalism as to the ability to accumulate and which should make it possible to increase the industrial output by roughly 75 per cent during the coming five years in spite of the exhaustion of the capacity reserves; strong emphasis on the possibility of developing "in an atmosphere of constant rapprochement between city and village, between proletariat and peasantry," [19] as one of the greatest advantages of Soviet industry. He did mention in a backhanded way what he termed the "shadowy aspects" of the Soviet economy such as "elements" of the goods famine, or the lack of reserves; yet these remarks contained no specific proposals for remedy but carried a clear implication that if people on the spot had applied themselves to their tasks with more zest, everything would be well. There was, however, no complacency in his remarks on agriculture, and here indeed something new was added. In view of the slowness of agricultural development, Stalin declared, the task of the party would now consist in bringing about "a gradual transition of pulverized peasant farms to the level of combined large-scale holdings, to the social collective cultivation of land on the basis of the intensification and mechanization of agriculture." [20] He was careful not to give any hint as to the anticipated speed of this movement, and, in an enunciation antedating his report to the Fifteenth Congress by a few weeks, he was explicit in emphasizing that it would take a long time to collectivize the bulk of the peasantry because such an undertaking would require "huge finances" which the Soviet state did not yet have at its disposal.[21] Still, his statement came as a surprise. But its true motives as well as its momentous implications were not to be revealed until later.

PART TWO

■ ▭ ■

The Issues and the Aftermath

VI

The Imbalance

PREOBRAZHENSKI'S analysis of the goods famine provides a convenient point of departure for our review of the debate. As will be recalled, his diagnosis which his opponents reluctantly accepted afterwards centered around the proposition that the Russian economy was thrown off balance by disturbances coming from two sides at once. Its capital stock was reduced. At the same time, the share of consumption in the national income rose sharply at the expense of compulsory as well as voluntary saving. In order to close this gap between the ability to produce and the level of demand, capacity had to increase by a substantial margin, particularly in the industrial sector which had suffered more than the rest and toward which the main pressure of the pent-up spending was now directed. This, in turn, called for a more than proportional increase in the lines producing the main components of this capacity, that is, in capital-goods industries. As long as a large reserve of underutilized plant was still in existence these tasks could be put off; after the end of this period of grace they could not be ignored any more.

This, in a nutshell, was the argument; and there is not a single step in it which does not make a good sense from the viewpoint of post-Keynesian economics. It is interesting, for example, to see Preobrazhenski's insistence on a shift toward investment seconded twenty years later by an outstanding British theorist with a remark that, in the period of postwar recovery, "it is *technically necessary* to employ

the increased labor force, now available, in making investment goods rather than consumption goods";[1] and it is
equally remarkable to note the parallels in the supporting
argument, with the Western economist lending force and
precision to the point about the exhaustion of the possibilities for output increases within the limits of existing capacity. Yet the similarity to present-day views is not confined
to emphasizing the desirability of substantial additions to
capital stock; it extends also to a presentation of the perils
inherent in such a policy. True, the Soviet economists of
the twenties failed to state explicitly the dichotomy between
the capacity-increasing and expenditure-generating effects
of investment. But as the account of their positions shows,
all the participants in the debate came around, in fact, to
recognizing these two effects and realized that while the
first of them would add to the stability of the Soviet economy,
the second would contribute to destabilization. In Preobrazhenski's words: "The systematic goods famine means
famine for new capital on the part of developing industry." [2]
Such a development could be presented easily in terms of
modern capital-stock adjustment theories and treated as a
case of the "overshoot" in which a move toward equilibrium
generates a move further away from equilibrium. The "famine
for new capital" can be conveniently put under the heading
of the acceleration principle; in fact, Preobrazhenski himself
came fairly close to providing a complete formula, without
using the term. And then it can be demonstrated that, given
appropriate values for the strategic variables, the inflationary
force of the expenditure effect is bound to gain momentum
and to bring about a grave disturbance before the salutary
capacity effect can assert itself.* It was this perspective that

* This corresponds, to be sure, only to one of the alternatives anticipated
for capitalist economy by neo-Keynesian theorists. It would be a situation
in which the expansionary forces would not permit the economy to slide off
the "ceiling" of full employment or full capacity but would be pushing it
head-on against these barriers. The stimulus to invest which would be

Bukharin and his friends were gravely concerned about. Preobrazhenski, on the contrary, was fearful lest the Soviet economy, owing to the timidity of its moderate leadership, should act more sluggishly than a full-blooded capitalist economy would. He warned, in effect, that it might refuse to follow through the logic of the acceleration principle by failing to raise the volume of investment in response to the increase in the final demand and by trying to keep down prices instead. To him, this meant getting the worst of the two worlds.* And while Preobrazhenski did not deny that the opposite course entailed serious risks, also, after adoption of the "forced saving" measures, he felt that the prize was sufficiently great to justify the gamble. Here, too, there are obvious analogies to the post-World War II situation in the West when theorists, having in common the basic conceptual framework and diagnosis of their countries' current economic ills, were nevertheless in sharp disagreement

---

powerful enough to do the trick would have to be an "autonomous" and not an "induced" one. It might be arguable whether in the conditions of the Soviet NEP the inflationary push of the strictly "induced" investment would not be much stronger than in a normal capitalist economy as a result of the higher marginal propensity to consume and the weaker "shift to saving" in the process of expansion. But as the reader can gather from all the foregoing, the Soviet economists never eliminated "autonomous" considerations from their discussions of investment policies, because, obviously enough, these considerations were, from the very beginning, of crucial importance for those in charge.

* "Under conditions of free competition, the disproportion [between the industrial production and the effective demand of the country] would be solved in the normal way, i.e. by the increase of prices in the lines of deficient output and the attendant increase in profits on capital invested in these lines which would immediately cause an influx of new capital, new construction, and eventually, an increase in output up to the level and possibly above the level of effective demand. . . . But let's assume that . . . the state [which owns 80 per cent of industry] fails to expand industrial output in accordance with the increase of effective demand. . . . We would [then] have (as we actually did have in 1925) an incompleted and hence utterly mutilated and distorted operation of the law of value because this law can cause an increase in prices on the retail level but is powerless to bring about, through the instrumentality of increased prices, a redistribution of the productive forces of the country in favor of faster industrialization." Preobrazhenski, *Novaya ekonomika*, pp. 196–197.

on the medicine to be applied. But little can be gained by pursuing these analogies further while remaining on the same level of generality. Such comparisons might make the particular points raised during the debate of the twenties more intelligible to the non-Soviet readers; they do not by themselves tell us whether the choices were in fact as grim as the above thumbnail sketch suggests. Was there real force behind the contention that the volume of investment should not be allowed to fall below some rock-bottom level which, while unspecified, was assumed to be high? Is it arguable that a goods famine in the Soviet economy of the twenties was bound to result in developments which would not fit into the conventional model of inflation but would be, if anything, even more disturbing? Our account of the debate has uncovered several specific attempts to answer these questions. It is now time to examine them in some detail.

◘

One attempt to dramatize the case for large-scale investment consisted in pointing to the arrears in the replacement of fixed capital over the period of the Civil War and the early years of the NEP. As was shown, it was Preobrazhenski and his left-wing friends who put the issue on the agenda and stressed its urgency while Bukharin at first seemed to assume that the policy of "unlocking the turnover" would take care of this problem as well as most others — only later did his position undergo a change. Yet neither side ever took the trouble to present its views on the subject in a systematic fashion. It seems therefore desirable to pursue the matter somewhat further.

To begin with, a few remarks on the quantitative aspects of the phenomenon are in order. None of the leading participants of the debate cited actual figures. Yet by the time that Preobrazhenski's book appeared, two authoritative attempts had been made to present the changes in capital stock over the period 1914–1923 by tabulating the estimated annual differences between gross investment and depreciation (in both instances depreciation was computed net of obsolescence). According to Professor Stanislav G. Strumilin, one of the leading statisticians of the Gosplan, the capital stock of Soviet large-scale industry in October 1924 was 11 per cent below its 1917 peak and 5 per cent above its prewar level.[3] The alternative set of estimates, published by the Central Statistical Administration presented a substantially different picture: 23 per cent decline from the 1917 peak and 12 per cent decline from the 1913 level by the end of 1924.[4] Considering all that is known about the respective computations, the second series appears more plausible; Strumilin seemed to understate the extent of the capital consumption in the years 1918–1924 and was not entirely convincing in his relatively high estimate of the increment in capital stock in the preceding period.[*]

Needless to say, in view of the formidable conceptual difficulties involved in measuring capital stocks it would be rash to accept any series of such kind even as the broadest

* More specifically, Strumilin's estimate of wear and tear seems exceedingly low; he put it at 2.9 per cent of the total value of the capital stock, and assumed it to be uniform over the whole period under consideration with no allowance made for the impact effects of virtual cessation of maintenance and repair activities during the Civil War and their woeful inadequacy in the early years of the NEP. (On the other hand, the idleness of a large part of capacity undoubtedly tended to counteract these debilitating effects by reducing the deterioration due to the normal use of plant. It is impossible to say whether the authors of the alternative series took this offset into account when they raised the estimated rate of wear and tear from 3.5 per cent in 1914–1917 to 5.5 per cent in 1918–1922/23.) Moreover, two steps in Strumilin's derivation of the increase in capital stock during the years 1914–1917 seem to involve an upward bias. The figure of the total output of civilian machinery given by him for these years is, for unknown reasons, considerably in excess of the figures contained in the cited source, and his assumption that the ratio between the increase of capital of the joint-stock companies and that of the total industrial capital was the same during the war and in the preceding period seems dubious in view of what is known about the marked increase in degree of concentration in the Russian industry during the war.

indication of the order of magnitude without looking around for corroborative evidence which would provide at least a rough external check. In the present case, fortunately, such an evidence is available. Time series which could be assumed, by and large, to move together with the investment volume and which were free of any index-number ambiguity showed a catastrophic decline during the period in question. The output of crude steel which had dropped by 1918 to ten per cent of its 1913 level, kept falling steadily through 1921 when it reached the low of five per cent of the prewar level and then climbed back to twenty-three per cent by 1924, with the pig iron and rolled-steel output series showing a nearly identical pattern.[5] Machinery imports which had amounted to more than a half of the apparent consumption in the prewar period dwindled to near zero during the Civil War.[6] And last but not least, the scattered data on the age composition of the Soviet industrial equipment during the midtwenties show a typical picture of an economy emerging from a deep slump in investment and climbing upward by borrowing heavily from the past. According to one of the most comprehensive surveys of the industrial power installations, the share of steam boilers and prime movers below ten years of age in the installed capacity totals of the two groups in 1925 was four and nine per cent, respectively. At the same time a very large portion of the power equipment in operation actually belonged on the scrap heap. The share of material exceeding in its age the normal service life, assumed to equal twenty to twenty-five years for both categories, amounted to about 50 per cent in the case of the steam boilers and about 30 per cent in the case of the prime movers.[7]

To conclude — the capital stock of the Soviet industry no doubt had been whittled down substantially. Did the existence of such arrears in replacement represent a valid argument in favor of a drastic increase in the rate of investment? Preobrazhenski and his friends were emphatic on this point, but they gave little explanation. They considered it a matter of course that once the possibilities of stepping up the utilization of the existing capacity were nearly exhausted, the arrears in replacement should be made up with utmost speed. As to the reasons, they did no more than stress that just as the failure to replace in the past had contributed to the goods famine of today, the continued reluctance to make up for this delay would lead to a goods famine of tomorrow. Yet while the analysis was skimpy, their judgment was essentially sound.

The first point to be made in support of the leftist view is a very conventional one. A reduction in the amount of capital in an economy within a given technological horizon implies (subject to qualifications to be discussed later on) an increase in its marginal returns, provided that the quantities of cooperating factors remained unchanged. The opportunities to invest, of course, must appear in a still more favorable light after the assumption of the given technological horizon has been relaxed. Preobrazhenski came very close to saying this when he talked about the "renewal of fixed capital in conditions of rapid technological progress," and he was clearly aware that this would apply to the Soviet economy no less than to capitalism. Here again a somewhat terse remark gains in clarity when it is spelled out a little. The choice between keeping an existing piece of equipment in service and replacing it by a new one is known to depend on the relationship between the operating costs associated with the use of the first and the total costs associated with the use of the second. In a situation where an abnormally large part of the existing equipment is antiquated and where the debilitating effects of old age are sharpened by prolonged undermaintenance, the stimulus to abandon existing equipment is operative with regard to a larger portion of total capital stock than in an economy with a younger and better-maintained industrial plant. Moreover, the highly advanced age of a relatively large portion of the stock implies that an unusually large crop of technological improvement must have matured over the average span of life of the existing equipment; and this must widen the spread in efficiency between the existing and the possible. Finally, extensive capital replacement permits the introduction of up-to-date equipment in the form of whole plants which can be fully and consistently organized in consonance with new methods; and this possibility, other things being equal, allows the economy to make a fuller use of potential increases in efficiency than in conditions of gradualist growth where new patterns are often introduced piecemeal. To be sure, "other things" are most unlikely to stay equal, and this makes the whole situation less clearcut. But let us postpone the discussion of these complexities until after another point in the case has been dealt with.

By pointing to the backlog of technological improvements, Preobrazhenski stressed the possibility of combining replacement and growth. He could have further strengthened his position by showing that the protracted period of capital consumption was bound to lift not only the upper limits for investment but also the floor, even if the technological changes had been entirely ignored. The reasons for this are not hard to find. The replacement demand is not merely a function of the size of its capital stock and of its average durability (complications arising from differences in durability of various kinds of equipment need not cause any serious difficulties). It depends also on the way in which this stock has been behaving in the past. In a stationary economy with a balanced age distribution of capital stock, the ratio of replacement to stock would obviously equal the reciprocal of the average durability of the existing plant. In a steadily growing economy this ratio would be lower than this reciprocal since the age group due for retirement at the end of the given year would be smaller than each of the remaining groups.* By the same token, in an economy which has been declining, the ratio of replacement to capital stock would have to exceed the reciprocal of the average durability if the decline should be arrested. The case of an economy whose capital stock has been successively growing, declining, and then growing again would clearly represent the combination of the last two patterns. It is this "intermediate" case, obviously enough, that fits best the Soviet situation of the twenties. The ratio of the replacement to stock immediately after resumption of growth might, or might not, have to be raised all the way so as to equal (or exceed) the reciprocal of the average durability; this would depend on the extent of underreplacement. But it will be definitely higher than it has been in the last year of the precontraction period because the size of the age group due for retirement has now grown, and the volume of the total capital stock has declined.†

In other words: a community which suffered a reduction in its capital stock would have to invest an amount of resources representing a larger fraction of its capital stock than before the shrinkage merely in order to maintain this stock on its reduced level. This would be significant enough, but it would be not the end of the story. First of all, the

* The extent of this divergence would be an increasing function of the length of the life span of the plant and of the rate of growth of the capital stock over the period equal to this life span. For a rigorous proof, as well as for an illuminating discussion of the whole problem see E. D. Domar, "Depreciation, Replacement and Growth," in *Essays in the Theory of Economic Growth* (New York, 1957), ch. vii.

† A simple numerical example may serve as an illustration. Let us consider an economy in which the capital stock K was growing up to a point at the rate r equalling 5 per cent per annum, with the average service life of the capital asset taken to be 10 years, the average construction period 1 year and the productive capacity of the equipment unit remaining intact until the time of retirement. Let us then observe the behavior of this capital stock during three successive stages (1) steady growth, (2) underreplacement taken to last three years during which the gross investment I amounts to a fraction of the retirement R, (3) resumption of the gross

"floor" would rather resemble an escalator; since the capital stock had been growing in the past, the size of the age groups due for retirement would keep increasing from one year to another. Moreover, a closer inspection of our model would reveal that such an "intermediate-case economy" would have to follow the injunction of the Queen in *Through the Looking Glass* in more than one respect. It would be impelled not only to run in order to stay put in the place

investment on a scale reflecting its precontraction ratio to the capital stock. The results are summarized in the table (all magnitudes are measured in units of productive capacity):

Year	I	R	I-R	K
1	100	61	39	806
2	105	64	41	847
3	110	67	43	890
4	116	70	46	936
5	122	74	48	984
6	128	78	50	1034
7	134	82	52	1086
8	141	86	55	1141
9	148	90	58	1199
10	155	95	60	1259
11	25	100	—75	1184
12	25	105	—80	1104
13	25	110	—85	1019
14	132	116	16	1035
15	134	122	12	1047
16	136	128	8	1055
17	137	134	3	1058
18	137	141	—4	1054
19	137	148	—11	1043
20	135	155	—20	1023
21	133	25	108	1131
22	147	25	122	1253

It can be easily seen that when

$$\frac{I_{10}}{K_{10}} = \frac{I_{14}}{K_{14}}; \frac{R_{10}}{K_{10}} < \frac{R_{14}}{K_{14}},$$

and that the same would hold true even if the shrinkage had lasted for no more than one year.

in which it found itself after the period of contraction, but also to run faster than before to make its capital stock recapture, and rise beyond, its previous peak at the same rate of speed at which it had been rising prior to the contraction, or at least at a rate not greatly inferior to the old. Otherwise the feedback effect between capital stock and investment would make itself felt in a rather disturbing manner. The steadily increasing volume of retirements would keep whittling down the size of net additions to stock. The resulting slackening in the increase in stock would in turn slow down the subsequent increase in total investment; and as the volume of retirements would continue to rise, the size of the net addition to stock would fall still further. Only the "replacement echo" of the lean years of contraction would break this cumulative deceleration. But it would set in only after a time period equal to the full life span of the plant; and even after this boost the rate of growth would still be below its precontraction level. (Actually, a contraction which had gone far enough to bring about a drastic decline in the ratio of net investment to replacement at the beginning of recovery, would not merely reduce the subsequent capital increments to utter insignificance; it could make them negative after a while, by letting the faster rise in volume of retirements overtake the slower rise in current investment also in absolute terms, until the "replacement echo" had put a stop to the relapse into shrinkage.) Yet even this somber picture can be viewed as too favorable on two counts. Thus far we assumed the average construction period of capital asset to equal one year, and individual assets were taken to maintain a constant level of productivity over their entire service life. But these assumptions do not always hold in real life, and our model would be seriously affected by their removal. A longer period of construction would require a larger amount of investment per annum in order to sustain a given rate of growth, and would make it more difficult to stop a contraction. Similarly, under conditions of the gradual decline of productivity of assets over time, it would be easier to whittle down the capital stock, and harder to restore it to the original level than in the case of constant productivity.* There can be little doubt

* A bit of elementary algebra and a moment of reflection should suffice to demonstrate the validity of these propositions:

(1) Let us assume that the average period of construction equals three years instead of one, with the total amount of resources needed for construction of individual assets and the average life span of the latter being the same as in the initial model. In order to satisfy the condition of steady increase in capital stock, the investment process would now have to be staggered; one part of the investment of the year (t) would complete the last third of the stock increment (k_t) due at the end of the same year, another part would produce the second third of the stock increment (k_{t+1}) due in year $(t+1)$, and the last part would contribute the first third of stock increment (k_{t+2}) due in year $(t+2)$. It should be evident that $\dfrac{K_t}{3} + \dfrac{K_{t+1}}{3} + \dfrac{K_{t+2}}{3} > K_t$ while in the case of a one year construction period the total investment is equal to the volume of completions. Moreover, in the initial model it was sufficient, in order to maintain the capital stock, to invest within each particular year the amount of resources equal to the amount invested n years earlier, no matter whether there was any drop in investment in the meantime or not. In the modified situation, the age group of capital assets going out of service during the first year after the contraction could not be fully replaced unless an adequate amount of resources had been invested during the preceding two years, but this would be impossible by definition.

(2) Let us assume that the productivity of individual assets is declining by constant absolute amounts per annum, with the volume of annual gross investments during the relevant time period and the average life span (n) of individual assets being the same as in the initial model. The replacement requirements would now be equal not to the full size of the oldest (and smallest) age group of the stock but to the sum total of the annual wear and tear of all the groups which had been in operation during the last service year of the oldest group; and since this wear and tear would amount to $\dfrac{1}{n}$ th of the total size of these (n) groups, it would be larger than in the case of discontinuous retirement. But while the replacement requirements would now be larger in absolute terms, the total capital stock would be, in the relevant sense, much smaller, with the cumulative wear and tear constituting the difference; the equal number of physical assets of the same kind would represent a smaller productive capacity. Consequently, equally large reduction of investment would cause a much sharper decline of the capital stock, both via uncompensated withdrawal of its oldest groups and via drastic rise in the average age of plant. The attempts to reverse the process by restoring the precontraction ratio of the total

that in the light of these amendments the situation of the Soviet economy in the midtwenties, with its notoriously long construction periods and woefully undermaintained plant, appears even less encouraging.

In sum, the restoration of the precontraction ratio between gross investment and capital stock seems exceedingly tenuous as a minimum condition for the resumption of growth. Yet this target, so modest compared to the needs, constitutes a highly exacting task when measured against capabilities. And here was another circumstance which Preobrazhenski and other discussants failed to mention, possibly because it was a matter of common knowledge. The sector which was to produce the wherewithal for the restoration of depleted stock suffered on balance much more heavily than the rest of the economy. To be sure, such an unevenness in decline was by no means inherent in the logic of the underreplacement process as such. On the contrary, the average durability of the physical plant in the capital-goods industries would probably be greater than in other lines. For this reason, a larger proportion of this plant would be likely to survive the period of negative net investment. Moreover, in Russia, as in most of the other countries participating in World War I the metal-working industries expanded well beyond their prewar level by 1916 in response to the pressing military needs.* Yet the debacle of 1917–1921 made the decisive difference. While the conversion of a more or less

investment to stock would be even less adequate than in the case of discontinuous retirement; indeed, the possibility of restoring this ratio would be problematical since shrinkage may have gone far enough to make such restoration a back-breaking task.

* According to the estimates of N. Ya. Vorob'ev, cited by S. G. Strumilin (*Ocherki* [1930], p. 100), the gross value of the output of machine-building plants covered by investigation rose from 308 million rubles in 1913 to 978 million rubles in 1916 (as measured in 1913 prices). Even if allowances are made for incompleteness of coverage and for a possible upward bias inherent in using initial-year prices as weights in period of rapid changes in composition of output, there can be no doubt that an impressive increase has occurred.

substantial part of the newly-built plant for the purposes of civilian production was undoubtedly possible also in the Soviet Union, the unusually large degree of general debilitation and of decline in skills made such a switch a very slow and costly proposition. But, however serious these difficulties may have been, they were overshadowed in importance by developments which have been mentioned earlier. The plunge of the output of ferrous metals to a near zero level reflected to a large degree, no doubt, the particular sensitivity of the iron and steel-making plant to disruption of transportation and to the shortage of mineral fuel. Yet one of the major factors behind this catastrophic drop was unquestionably the decline in fixed capital which had been caused by extensive destruction in addition to massive undermaintenance and which went far beyond the all-industry average, owing to accidents of military-political geography; the Civil War raged with particular ferocity in the southwestern regions where the bulk of the Soviet iron and steel industry was located. According to authoritative estimates, the net capital stock of the Soviet ferrous metallurgy amounted at the end of 1925 to no more than two-thirds of its prewar volume.[8]

Did this reduction in the Soviet capital-making capacity imply that the stimuli to expand (coming from the demand side) and the obstacles to expansion (coming from the supply side) would be simultaneously reinforced? The participants of the debate never faced squarely this aspect of the situation: yet it was disturbingly real. Indeed, if the underreplacement had been particularly drastic in some areas on which the operation of the whole system decisively depended, and if some significant economies of scale had been lost in the process, the whole economy might well have been pushed back into the range of increasing returns, a state of affairs which should generate very powerful inducements to invest. At the same time the heavy damage done to the capital-goods industries would cause a steep increase in the cost of investment. In terms used by Professor Abba P. Lerner,[9] while the marginal productivity of capital would now be relatively high and rising, the marginal efficiency of investment would be low and sharply declining. To make things worse, a larger share of the total output of the capital-goods' industries would now have to be directed, for reasons set forth in earlier paragraphs, toward maintaining the capital at its reduced level. Theoretically speaking, the attempts toward recovery could be checkmated as a result; the shrinkage of the capital-goods capacity as a compounded effect of underreplacement, undermaintenance and outright destruction might go so far as to make the cost of reconstruction approach infinity (e.g., if all steel-producing plants had been razed to the ground). In a slightly less extreme case, the marginal efficiency of investment would approach zero at a level of output of capital goods which would be less than sufficient to make good the relatively expanded replacement requirements; as a result, the shrinkage would continue, and the economy would be heading toward ultimate collapse just as in the previous case, although more slowly.

There is surely no reason to assume that the actual situation of the Soviet economy of the twenties corresponded to this dismal picture. Moreover, if the schedule of the marginal efficiency of investment can be taken to show positive values also beyond the replacement level, the gains to be attained from pushing down its slope would be unusually great. The further such push would go, the faster would the economy be moving along the rising schedule of the marginal productivity of capital. And this, in turn, would mean that the schedules of the marginal efficiency of investment would be shifting upward and becoming flatter as long as the capital-goods industries kept recapturing the lost economies of scale in the process of expansion as well as assimilating the improvement in technology which had occurred in the meantime.* Yet this would be only one part of the story. To set the volume of investment at a comparatively high level in spite of steeply rising costs would imply a correspondingly low (explicit or virtual) rate of interest — a much lower one, no doubt, than would correspond to the voluntary time preference of the population. An authority which would attempt to act on the basis of its own time-preference schedule and to carry this volume of

* A three-dimensional diagram borrowed with slight modifications from Lerner's *Economics of Control* (p. 336), may illustrate the point.

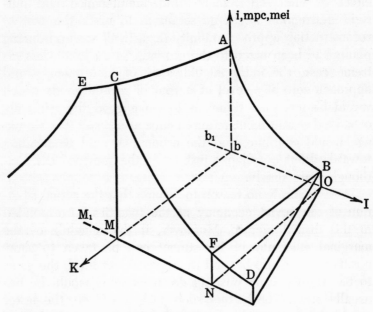

The horizontal lines bK and bI represent the amount of capital and the rate of net investment, respectively, while the vertical line bR measures marginal productivity of capital, marginal efficiency of investment, and the rate of interest. The dotted lines b_1b and M_1M show the rate of replacement necessary to maintain the capital at the level of b and M. Point E indicates the end of the range of increasing returns to capital. It can be easily noted that as long as the economy moves within this range, FN is larger than BO while bO equals MN.

investment across, would be in for heavy weather. Giving a high priority to rebuilding the capital-intensive heavy industries would imply the tying up of large amounts of resources in projects which would not start giving off output flows until after several years. Preobrazhenski, it will be recalled, stated this in so many words. He was equally explicit in pointing out that the necessity of "discontinuous shift" was closely linked with the transition from the "restoration" to "reconstruction" and with the legacy of underreplacement. True, there were no reasons to assume that the difference between these two stages would be of a razor-edge quality. It was still possible to move ahead here and there by stepping up the utilization of existing capacity, and stretching the life span of equipment still further beyond the time limit of "normal" retirement. In fact, Preobrazhenski himself admitted the possibility of such "borrowing from the total stock of fixed capital" in his discussion of the postwar developments in capitalist economies.[10] But attempts to make use of all these ways of mending and making do would involve, as Bazarov put it, "greater and steadily increasing efforts," in other words — a steep increase in costs. And while the resulting lag of the increase in supply behind the increase in outlays would be less formidable than if full-dress investment in fixed capital had been pushed all the way down the line, it would be serious enough to generate strong inflationary pressures.

◙

Our analysis of the perils of protracted underreplacement has ended in the discussion of the dangers lurking behind the attempts to make it good. Yet the changes on the capacity side represented, as it were, only one blade of the scissors. The other was related to the changes in the size and structure of national income. With regard to this problem area the Soviet economists of various groups were much more articulate and forthright, if brief, in stating the essential points.

To begin with, the leftist Preobrazhenski and the middle-of-the-roader Bazarov were quite explicit in stressing the decline in the potential for voluntary saving as a result of the revolution. Moreover, in contradistinction to the spokesmen on the official line, from Stalin down, they did not seem to attach much importance to reduction of luxury consumption as a compensating factor under Soviet conditions. Preobrazhenski did not mention it at all, and Bazarov was openly skeptical. All this amounted to saying that the propensity to consume would now be much closer to unity than before 1917, even if the real income per capita had been restored to its earlier level (which was clearly not the case in the midtwenties). This state of affairs, in conjunction with the developments discussed before, would result in a highly explosive situation. The multiplier effect of the new investment would be strong; yet it would have to spend itself largely in price increases or (in case of repressed inflation) in rising excess demand. Idle plant which might absorb the impact of increased spending was strictly limited. Owing to systematic depletion of the capital stock during the preceding period, the bottleneck level would be uncomfortably close at a relatively early stage of recovery. Lastly, the nature of the relevant time lags would be not propitious for stability. As a result of high pent-up demand and lack of confidence in the value of money, the lag in spending would tend to be inordinately short. Yet the gestation period of the plant would be, because of the rundown condition of the capital-goods industries and of the sluggishness of the constructional work, inordinately long. Preobrazhenski's assumption that the construction of an average plant would require three to four years did not seem to be wide of the mark, at any rate — for the capital-goods industries. And this would mean that while the expenditure effect of investment would be quick and powerful, the capacity effect would be painfully slow in coming.

Up to this point our discussion appears to have gone full circle. We are, it would seem, once again confronted with a case of an inflation which is fairly typical even if rather unusually grave. Yet the Soviet analyses of the goods famine contained, in addition to the familiar considerations set forth above, also a novel aspect.

In a modern industrialized economy the interdependence of its various parts is a two-way affair. However broadly or however narrowly an "industry" is defined, its scale of operation will always depend on the supplies from the rest of the economy at least as much as the scale of operations of the rest of the economy will depend on the supplies from this particular "industry." The situation is very different whenever modern manufacturing and mining exist side by side with a backward and overpopulated peasant agriculture. While the first cannot function at all without a certain minimum of supplies from the second, the latter can, although at the price of a more or less considerable drop in output, remain in operation without supplies from the first. In contradistinction to the mechanized farming of advanced countries, the primitive peasant agriculture could counter the loss of supplies in manufactured goods by stretching the utilization of available equipment to the limits of physical endurance and by increasing the reliance upon the production of nonfarm consumers goods as well as of some agricultural implements in peasant households. While the substitution of handmade wooden hoes for steel ploughs would entail a drop in agricultural yields, it would certainly not involve a cessation of production.

In times of critical shortages of manufactured goods such

a state of things could have definite advantages for the industrial segment of the economy. A determined policy of confiscating the agricultural surplus with practically no counterflows of goods from the cities need not under such conditions lead purely mechanically, i.e. by sheer lack of necessary factor inputs, to an immediate collapse of agricultural production. Such was, in essence, the situation in the period of War Communism. And such was (to a much attenuated degree, of course) also the state of affairs before the revolution when the compulsion to sell without buying on anything like a comparable scale was firmly built into the institutional setup of Russian agriculture — Preobrazhenski, it will be recalled, made this one of his central points. After the War Communist apparatus of compulsory saving had followed its Tsarist predecessor on the way to the scrap heap, things changed fundamentally, but not at once. In between there was a period of grace which made possible the miracle of the early NEP and which influenced profoundly the thinking of the party economists. By unlocking the resources of small-scale industry, the state was in a position to step up supplies to the villages. The peasants who had been starved of these supplies for many years responded with a marked increase in the amount of foodstuffs and raw materials available to the cities and were willing to put up with the "tax in kind" which represented, from their point of view, a vast improvement over the ruthlessly confiscatory policies of the earlier period. The bulk of the proceeds of this tax and at least a portion of the food surpluses passing through the private market could then be channelled to the large-scale industries to set some of its idle wheels into motion. A genuine cumulative process was started with increases in urban supplies trickling down to the countryside and calling forth further increases in counterflows from agriculture. These, in turn, provided necessary wherewithals for another round of gains in industrial output, and the same process might, on the face of it, continue on and on along a steadily rising spiral. It was, in a way, a sort of multiplier effect operating not from the side of demand but from the side of supply, with the amount of marketable agricultural surplus playing the role of the good old-fashioned "wage fund" in determining the volume of employment.

When Bukharin and his friends saw the situation in such light they were certainly not day-dreaming. Moreover, their most formidable opponent never denied the substantial element of truth in their analysis. Preobrazhenski fully realized that "the extent of accumulation [in socialist sector] depends on the extent of exchange" between industry and agriculture,[11] and he was emphatic in stressing that the policy of monopolistic squeeze should not be pushed too far. Yet he was right in assuming that the Soviet economy in its present state could not sustain such a "balanced growth" much longer. The approach of capacity limits would mean that industrial supply curves which had been until now obligingly flat were now to turn sharply upward. The basis for a policy of closing the scissors between industrial and agricultural prices would be effectively destroyed thereby. To be sure, supply curves could be shifted to the right by an increase in capacity large enough to meet the pressure of the steadily growing demand — a task made more formidable by the underreplacement policies of the preceding years. Yet everyone agreed by 1926 that such an addition to the capacity would absorb a much larger volume of resources per unit of output, and involve a longer gestation process than expansion of the "restoration" variety. True, given a determined effort to squeeze the utmost from the existing plant, the output of industrial consumers goods need not necessarily decline in process. But a much larger share of it would now go to the rapidly growing urban labor force whose real earnings were higher than those of agricultural producers.* At the same time the demand for food on the part of this labor force would grow at least *pari passu* with its increase if not faster. It would be at this juncture that the ominous potentialities of the backward agriculture would become operative. The peasant faced with tapering-off supply of industrial goods and with increasing claims for his own products would simply refuse to play the game. He would be increasingly reluctant to increase his market-able output even under the old terms of trade after having reached (in Bazarov's words) "the level of the absolutely indispensable" in his consumption of industrial products. It would be therefore perfectly logical for him to respond to the turn for the worse by reducing his marketings and taking a long step backward to the self-contained *Naturalwirtschaft.* The fact that the peasant had been able to replenish some of the most glaring gaps in his capital stock during the pre-ceding years would strengthen his hand in this maneuver. As a result, the urban sector of the economy would not merely experience a lag in output behind the demand but an actual decline in supply of goods representing the key item in workers' consumption as well as in the exports designed to procure the much needed equipment from abroad. The profoundly disruptive effect of such a situation would be too obvious to elaborate on, and it would be a matter of relatively minor importance whether the train of ominous events would start out under the guise of a goods famine rather than of an open inflation.

* Preobrazhenski strongly implied this when he insisted that "the increase in the wage fund of workers in the light industry . . . *should precede* the increase in satisfying the peasant demand for consumers goods produced by the state-owned light industry" (*VKA*, XXII, p. 65). He was even more outspoken when he spurned peasant protests against wage increases and declared that "socialism knows only one kind of equalization of the material conditions in city and countryside; and this equalization consists, if temporary improvements in the position of small-scale producers are dis-regarded, in the liquidation of the very foundations of the small-scale pro-duction" (*ibid.,* p. 64).

A somewhat unconventional version of the standard Marshallian diagram may be of help in presenting parts of the argument of the last section in a more systematic fashion. The value of the construct, it goes without saying, is primarily didactic. It involves a number of assumptions which while not implausible, cannot be accepted without a thoroughgoing statistical test. In their present form they should be treated, at best, as suggestive hypotheses.

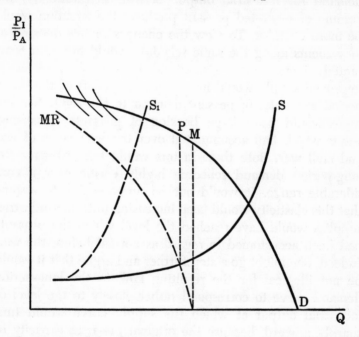

The Y axis of the diagram measures the ratio of industrial to agricultural prices, the X axis — the volume of industrial output available to the peasants. In view of ample capacity reserves in the urban sector at the beginning of the recovery, the S-curve could be expected to be fairly flat over the wide range of outputs open to the economy. Furthermore, since investments in fixed capital were insignificant during the initial years, it would not be illegitimate to treat the increase of output over time during the early period as a movement along the same supply schedule rather than as a shift of this schedule to the right. It would be possible, however, to have an initial onceover shift of such a kind even without investment in an industry emerging from chaotic conditions of a civil war.

With regard to the D-curve representing the peasant demand for industrial output as well as (indirectly) the volume of marketed peasant produce, the situation would be more complex. To view the changes in this demand as movements along the same schedule would not seem warranted: increases in agricultural income as a result of improved supply would involve a steady shift of the short-period schedules of peasant demand to the right. Besides, there would be a large backlog of peasants' unsatisfied wants which had accumulated over the lean years of war and civil war. Both these factors would tend to make the long-period demand schedule highly elastic over a considerable range. It would not be unreasonable to assume that this elasticity would keep increasing until the industrial supplies would have reached the level which the peasants had been accustomed to regard as normal before the war. Indeed, one might go a step further and argue that it would be not illogical for the resulting kink in the long-period demand curve to correspond rather closely to the level of industrial output at which the supply curve would turn sharply upward, because the original pre-1914 capacity of industries supplying the peasant market would be presumably rather well adjusted to its size. (It should be obvious, incidentally, that the kink in the demand curve would denote the maximum volume of peasant marketings.)

To the extent that these assumptions would hold, some of Bukharin's early arguments would undoubtedly gain in cogency. He sounded unnecessarily categorical when he asserted that "with lower prices but greater volume of sold commodities . . . it is possible to get a larger volume of profits." [12] He seemed, moreover, to contradict himself or to be evasive when he argued, on another occasion, that "it would be nonsense on our part to refuse to exploit our monopolistic position; but we should limit this exploitation in order not to restrict but to enlarge the absorptive capacity of our internal market . . ." [13] Yet in the light of all the foregoing, these loosely-worded statements seemed to add up quite well. It was entirely legitimate to argue that the administrators of the Soviet industry in the summer of 1923 had set the price ratio between industry and agriculture at the level which, speaking in terms of our diagram, made them land to the left of the maximum-profit point P. Furthermore, it would stand to reason that, with the cost curve being low as well as flat over a wide range of industrial output, the monopoly point would be closer to the point of maximum agricultural supply than in case of the steeply rising curve. A glance at the hypothetical S'-curve of our diagram would confirm this. Consequently, the extent of monopolistic deviation from what a Western theorist would consider optimum would be effectively reduced. It could be argued, of course, that even a small deviation would be unjustifiable and that prices should be set at the level of marginal costs. Such an idea, not unnaturally, never crossed the mind of Bukharin, nor of any other Soviet economist of that period. But even if they had been aware of the "rule," they could still attempt to justify their deviant policies by pointing out that an accelerated industrial growth was in the long run beneficial for the economy as a whole, and that possibilities of reshuffling resources from agriculture to industry by the way of direct taxation or voluntary peasant savings were severely limited. (Besides, the Soviet economists reasoned in terms of average costs; and since marginal costs would be above average costs as soon as the latter would begin to rise, a part of what Bukharin and other debaters considered a monopolistic markup would be a component of a *bona fide* competitive price.) Bukharin's reluctance to renounce the advantages of a monopolistic position would appear vindicated thereby. At the same time his warnings against using these advantages to the limit would still make good sense, if interpreted as an advice to settle down to the right of P (or even of M). It was not unrealistic to expect during the early period of the NEP that an improvement in the supply of implements and of industrial consumers goods to the peasants would result in larger agricultural marketings a year hence, and that this increase would be sufficiently great to justify the present-year's sacrifice involved in relaxation of monopolistic squeeze.

But while our construct makes it possible to present Bukharin's ideas in a somewhat more coherent way it also throws into sharp relief their limitations. Bukharin failed to make provisions for developments beyond the near-horizontal range of the supply curve. He paid no attention to the fact that, owing to the massive underreplacement of the past years, this range would be most likely to end at the lower level of output than it would have been possible if this reduction in capacity had not occurred. He ignored the possibility of a kink in the peasant demand curve; and he gave no indication of noticing that while the physical havoc caused by the revolution resulted in shifting the supply curve to the left, the concomitant upheaval in income distribution had the effect of moving the peasant demand curve to the right. In all these respects Preobrazhenski showed a better insight than his chief adversary.

VII
Relaxation Possibilities

In the preceding chapter we attempted to present in a systematic fashion the main elements of the Soviet economic situation in the midtwenties as they emerged from the controversy. Our discussion did not make the circumstances which underlay the debate seem any the less dramatic. On the contrary, it underscored the gravity of the basic dilemma by bringing into sharper focus the critical nature of the key variables and the ominous way in which they hung together. The same facts of the situation which pushed toward a large volume of investment made such an increase dangerous for economic stability; and the peasants' readiness to meet an inflationary disturbance by a massive withdrawal from the market threatened to bring the Soviet economy back to the brink of disaster where it had been on the eve of the NEP. Yet it would be rash to proceed from here to ultimate conclusions without taking a closer look at the macroeconomic aggregates we have been dealing with up to now. Could not a way out be found through some manipulation of the intersectoral structure of investment which would secure higher over-all returns for the given volume of outlays? Also what of the capital intensity within the different sectors — could not the investment requirements be scaled down if this intensity were effectively reduced?

As our account of the debate has shown, its participants were not unaware of these questions. The most unqualifiedly affirmative answer came from Shanin. The reader will recall that he recommended giving priority to investment projects of low capital intensity, more particularly — to investment in labor-intensive agriculture in preference to the more capitalistic industrial sector, and, within the latter, to the consumers goods rather than to producers-goods industries. To the Western-trained economist of our day ideas of this kind undoubtedly have a familiar ring. They have been put forward since the early forties by a number of eminent theorists trying to devise appropriate investment criteria for underdeveloped countries. But while the Soviet reaction to Shanin's proposal was, with very few exceptions, rich in invective and poor in argument, the rate-of-turnover criterion of Western economists has met a number of effective criticisms which would fully apply to Shanin's position as well.[1] Most of these criticisms, as will be shown later on, acquire added significance when viewed in the perspective of long-range growth. They might, however, be briefly sketched at the present stage of our discussion:

(1) An obvious weakness of the Shanin approach consists in focusing on the relation between output and *only one* factor of production. Some of the methods which require relatively little capital per unit of output use up prodigiously large amounts of labor. They may therefore turn out to be more resource consuming even under conditions of a very pronounced scarcity of capital unless labor's supply price is taken to be zero — an assumption which cannot be taken seriously even in the situation of large-scale unemployment. Moreover, while the factor side of the calculation is not complete, the output side is overstated. To view larger gross returns as an indicator of the higher productivity of capital implies not only a disregard of the fact that these gross returns reflect contribution of non-capital factors as well but also a failure to account for differences in longevity. Since important lines of production with comparatively high capital/output ratios happen to use highly durable plants,

they require comparatively low replacement and maintenance expenditures in relation to initial outlay. Consequently, many of these projects may wind up with a high ratio of *net* return to capital not only on account of a saving on labor but also because of the reduction of replacement and maintenance costs, and some of them may retain this superiority also after the appropriate rate of interest has been brought into picture. The rate-of-turnover criterion, consistently applied, is unable to take this into account.

(2) Shanin as well as most of his Western counterparts showed a distinct inclination to treat the capital/output ratio and capital/labor ratio as closely interrelated and broadly interchangeable. Such an attitude is justified with regard to a single industry which can produce any given amount of its product with a variety of combinations of capital and labor and in which the proportional increase in all factors would lead to an equiproportional increase in output (the so-called "homogeneous production function of first degree"). Yet it is out of place with regard to an economy as a whole which obviously consists of a large number of industries with production functions of widely different shapes. The same capital/output ratios (or the same marginal productivities of capital, for that matter) may go together with widely diverging factor proportions in particular industries. The point seems trite but it is not unimportant. It shows the limitations of the view according to which an economy poorly endowed with capital should spread its investment (or the bulk of it) judiciously thin over the vast amounts of available labor, and the point is further strengthened when we stop thinking in terms of these two factors alone. A capital-poor country may be abundantly endowed with natural resources which, for compelling technological reasons, can be exploited only in a heavily capital-using way. On the other hand, while in some parts of such an economy there are powerful forces pushing for a

large minimum size of capital outlays, in other areas the limitations on application of capital are more severe than can be explained merely by the prevailing capital/labor ratio. An agriculture, unable to use implements above a certain size owing to the extreme fragmentation of the land is a case in point. The fact that at the same time there is a considerable waste of capital locked up in housing facilities and in working livestock complicates the picture still further. (It may be pointed out, in addition, that in view of the unaugmentable nature of the factor "land," the capital/output ratio in agriculture tends to increase over time relatively to the capital/output ratio in the urban sector, and that this tendency is likely to gain momentum as the margin of cultivation within the settled area draws close. Yet such an upward trend in the capital/output ratio comes in response to the mounting pressure of a growing population against the available land, and therefore belongs more properly in a discussion of long-term developments.) Even a superficial look at the Soviet economy of the midtwenties reveals the presence of these uncomfortable characteristics.

(3) The situation outlined above is entirely possible also if all individual production functions are of an homogeneous first-degree variety and if particular isoquants, showing the alternative ways of producing outputs of a given size, are obligingly continuous. Yet such assumptions, conservatively speaking, have no universal validity. The range of choices may consist, in many instances, of discreet points. Indivisibilities are likely to be present and to attain, in spots, considerable importance from the viewpoint of the economy as a whole, particularly when enmeshed in a system of pronounced complementarity relations. This is, to repeat, what Preobrazhenski seemed to have in mind when he spoke of "chain connection." It is not difficult to show that these considerations might carry more weight whenever changes in the economy are large and abrupt. If returns are taken to

be variable, and if the assumption of the first degree homogeneity is relaxed, a community that has experienced a substantial reduction in its capital stock can be visualized as sliding down to a level at which it will show a lower marginal (as well as average) social productivity of capital because some significant economies of scale have been lost — a possibility which has already been mentioned in another context. Hence the return to the original position would entail an increase in returns to capital.* This tendency will be compounded if the decline in stock has been not only drastic but uneven to the point of disrupting some fundamental complementarity relationships so that there is little room left for substitution, at least in the short run. To the extent that the most affected areas can contain a relatively small number of large units, the additions to stock have to be lumpy in order to be effective. Concretely, the reduction of capital stock in the highly concentrated and tightly integrated Soviet steel industry by one-third unavoidably involved a loss of certain economies of scale. Moreover, in view of the strategic position of this industry, its return to full capacity was bound to have powerful repercussions

---

* A moment of reflection will show that the same proposition could be put in a slightly different way and still be compatible with fairly orthodox assumptions. The "comparative statics" approach works with situations when the capital stock of the economy is fully adjusted in its technological shape to the prevailing scarcity relationships as reflected in relative factor prices. Each of these setups could be taken to contain a number of heavily capitalistic industries which were from the viewpoint of their total contribution to social product distinctly inframarginal, but while the amount of producer's surplus per given volume of invested resources would be in these industries above average, they would have pushed their expansion all the way to the point at which their marginal social productivity would be equal to the one prevailing in other uses. Suppose now that the economy in question was subjected to partial destruction due to an exogenous development such as war, and that this destruction affected all lines to the same extent. (For the Soviet case, the last assumption would not be true, as was shown in the previous chapter, but let us disregard this.) Given all this, it would be entirely legitimate to conclude that the marginal productivity of investment in the inframarginal areas would now be larger than in the rest of the economy.

throughout the system, by reducing the costs of its supplies to the other lines and by increasing its own demand for their outputs — a typical case of what Professors Viner and Scitovsky called "pecuniary external economies." [2]

(4) The benefits to be derived from such resumption of advance, however, would be larger than the foregoing suggests. The new investment need not represent a mere repetition of the old pattern; nor does it need to lie within the same technological horizon. And here we come to another point which has been alluded to before: a country which undergoes an interruption in its investment activities while the rest of the world keeps advancing is bound to be confronted at the end of this period with an unusually large family of new production functions. Under such conditions the gap in productivity between the new and the old will be larger than in case of continuous uninterrupted development; and up-to-date methods will show an edge over a correspondingly broader range of choices, also when their adoption entails a substitution of scarce capital for abundant labor. Such a probability will be particularly pronounced wherever the technological progress has occurred not by slow motion but by rapid spurts. This was in fact the situation in the West during the first post-World War I decade.

(5) Among the diverse points brought up in the preceding paragraphs Shanin himself explicitly mentioned and conceded one. He qualified his argument in favor of a low capital/output ratio by pointing out that a large-sized (and highly capital-intensive) railroad system was a necessary prerequisite also for the smooth development of those lines which he wanted to promote in the first place. Bazarov attempted to widen the crack in his opponent's armor when he noted that by the same token heavy industries whose supplies were indispensable for the construction and operation of transportation facilities should be given a correspondingly high share in the total investment volume. In

another connection, Bazarov and Preobrazhenski pressed the point still further by emphasizing the dependence of small-scale farming on developments in nonagricultural areas of the economy. And both of them made it quite clear that this dependence operated through strictly technological complementarity as well as, more indirectly, through stronger inducement to agricultural investment due to larger markets for farm goods, and a more abundant supply of industrial goods to the countryside. They could have added that a reduction in the amount of the agricultural over-population would strongly operate in the same direction by raising the peasants' incentives for efficient working and their readiness to adopt better farming methods — a point which has been made more than once in recent literature.

Yet even if all the considerations set forth in the preceding paragraphs had been summarily dismissed, Shanin's rudimentary model with its ingeniously contrived compounding effect would still be open to another objection. It treated the relationship between two large segments of the economy in strictly microeconomic terms, and it ignored the fact that in the case on hand this relationship involved also complementarity and not merely substitutability. While today's steel would compete with today's grain for investable resources, its expansion would help to produce more grain tomorrow. In terms of Shanin's numerical example, the continuous reinvestment into agriculture of the initial amount of 100 as well as of its annual increments would mean that the claim for the output of the capital-goods industry on the part of agriculture would rise from 100 in the first year to 115 in the second, 132 in the third, and 152 in the fourth. He did not seem to notice that the resulting increases in agricultural output would go at the expense of the expansion of the capacity of the capital-goods industry, and, consequently, of the higher potential increase in agricultural output in the more distant future; the importance of the distinction between capital goods producing flows of consumable goods and those producing additions to the social capital stock obviously escaped him at this point. The shift of resources to industry which Shanin proposed to carry out after four years and which presumably implied a sudden reduction of agricultural investment to the level at which it stood prior to the assigning of the original 100 to agriculture, would be of limited significance. A transfer of this kind could, at its best, restore to capital-goods industry the resources which had gone into agricultural investment since the beginning of the whole operation; it could provide no compensation for the loss of additions to the capital-making capacity which these resources would have produced if they had not been diverted to agriculture.*

In the specific conditions of the Soviet twenties the consequences of Shanin's policies were particularly grave. To refrain from large investment in capital-goods industries which had just stopped contracting would mean to risk a relapse into shrinkage. And the impact of this shrinkage would be fairly immediate since the curtailed sector, taken as a whole, by no means had been oversized with regard to the rest of the economy prior to its decline. To sum up: in an economy in which the capital-using sector is complementary to the noncapitalistic sector in more than one sense, and at the same time barely sufficient to sustain the current

---

* It might be argued that our criticism of Shanin's view is less than fair because (1) a poor community would be under no obligation to aim at maximization of its long-run rate of economic growth; (2) fixing the investment in agriculture (and/or in consumers goods in general) below a certain level would backfire against the output of capital goods by reducing the productivity of labor; (3) the given amount of investment in agriculture would consist, in large parts, of resources which would be neither products nor significant inputs of capital-goods industry (fodder for livestock, for instance). But the first proposition would be of little use to Shanin who did argue in favor of maximizing the long-run rate of growth and claimed that his method was most appropriate for this purpose. The second was not questioned by anyone, as will be seen presently. And the third would mean that the problem of choice between agricultural and heavy industrial investment would be, up to a point, less acute than Shanin seemed to imply.

level of operation of the whole system, the policy of curtailing the first is bound to boomerang against the second before long. The macroeconomic considerations slip in, as it were, through the rear door of the "chain connection" in order to prevent the attempts at relaxation from going overboard.

◘

To criticize Shanin's proposals is by no means to advocate that the Soviet economy should have swung all the way in the opposite direction; and none of the ranking participants of the debate ever suggested anything like that. The most intrepid protagonist of bigness and speed indignantly declared that "nobody suggests such economic illiteracy as mortgaging all resources for development of heavy industry." * Moreover, in a remark preceding the ringing "chain connection" paragraph, he observed that "accumulation is needed for the state economy to reach the level of the new capitalist economy *whenever it is impossible to approximate the level of the new technology gradually.*" [3] This implicitly admits that the range of choice between alternative methods of production is wider in some fields than in others and that these differences should be utilized. The concern about these differences would surely not have arisen without a realization that an economy which is poor in capital has to find a way to ration this critically scarce factor even if the Shanin type of surgery is rejected as too reckless. As readers may recall, it was Bazarov who came

* "Ekonomicheskie zametki," part II, *B* (March 31, 1926), p. 68. The immediately following sentence was even more emphatic: "We need a proportional development of heavy and light industry." "Proportional" meant here presumably "balanced" or "simultaneous" — otherwise the cited statement would be clearly inconsistent with many other passages in Preobrazhenski's writings which stressed the need for faster growth of capital-goods industry. Yet while the wording of the proposition is questionable, it clearly shows an inclination to keep the disparity in growth rates rather limited.

closest to saying this in so many words. More than that — it was Bazarov who made a most determined effort to devise a system of policies which would use up to the hilt the possibilities of relaxation wherever they existed in order to spare the maximum amount of resources for assignments not admitting of such possibilities. The specific suggestions he made have been set forth at some length in Part One. It will suffice to restate in all brevity those which are most pertinent here:

(1) Bazarov did not try to skirt the problem of the replacement of fixed capital, and he was emphatic in voicing his concern about the archaic quality of a large portion of the Soviet industrial plant. Yet he took note of the fact that between pushing the utilization of existing capacity into the range of steeply-rising cost and full-dress new investment there was an intermediate solution such as partial reconstruction. This would entail limited additions to plant or replacement of some parts of equipment which were worn out more than others or which could be discarded most profitably and most easily in favor of more up-to-date material. He was aware that such a solution might be inferior in terms of long-run efficiency to a full-scale reconstruction. Indeed, Western readers (although probably not the less scarcity-conscious Soviet audience of his day) might feel that he apologized too much for the "irrationality" of such outlays and for the impossibility of "making only such investments which appear rational from the viewpoint of the general plan." On the other hand, Bazarov could have pointed out that the comparative disadvantages of the partial reconstruction methods would be in some lines more pronounced than in others, owing to the higher degree of integration of plant or to the "single-package" nature of the improvement in question. In any event Bazarov undoubtedly succeeded in demonstrating that inbetween solutions might make the switch from the "period of restoration" to the "pe-

riod of reconstruction" less abrupt and less costly than some of the leftist pronouncements assumed. Moreover, a quick glance at the figures shows that this intermediate category accounted, in fact, for a very large fraction of the total investment in Soviet industry during the last years of the NEP.*

(2) The problem of appropriate factor proportions was tackled in a similar fashion. No doubt, whenever Bazarov attempted to set up something like a general criterion, he was none too successful. It will be recalled that he favored the use of methods requiring more labor in combination with the given amount of capital only when they would yield a higher output per worker, and perforce also per unit of capital. This was surely too exacting a condition. Moreover, and not unlike the rate-of-turnover rule, Bazarov's solution failed to take into account the durability of investment. A bit of plain arithmetic shows that if the method requiring more labor per given amount of capital were assumed to show smaller output per worker and the durability of capital were to be equal in both cases, the low durability would result in a lower cost per unit for the labor-intensive method while high durability would favor the second alternative. In fact, this extremist formula was worse than useless for Bazarov's purposes. He did not need it in order to prove that in important areas of the economy a technology which maximizes employment is (at least for outputs above certain

* According to an authoritative Soviet source, the share of "extension and reequipment" of old plants in the total investment in the state industry was 55.2 per cent in 1925/26, 56.1 per cent in 1926/27, and 55.7 per cent in 1927/28 (B. Gukhman, "Na rubezhe," *PKh* (1928) no. 8, p. 136). Some of these investments which aimed at "better utilization of the whole old production frame" were said to involve "very serious reconstruction of the old plant." This would presumably bring them closer to the "new construction" category which rose from 12.3 to 26.3 per cent of the total over the same period. On the other hand, allowance would have to be made for the "capital repair" type of investment which was not included in the "reconstruction" category and which amounted, respectively, to 19.4, 13.3, and 9.7 per cent of the total investment during the same three years (*ibid.*).

size) economically inferior to labor-saving alternatives even under conditions of the extreme scarcity of capital, and should be rejected if maximization of output is to be the guiding principle. Yet he was fully aware that what held true in some sectors of the economy, did not apply to others. He insisted that in lines where possibilities of substituting labor for capital over the whole relevant range of output were broader, the application of labor-intensive methods should be pushed all-out, undeterred by a predilection for modernity or by the union regulations. Moreover, the complementarity factor which served thus far to disprove the overenthusiastic notions about opportunities for "cheap" investment could now be turned around in order to reveal its more cheerful side. A capital-poor community could use large quantities of its abundant labor armed with rudimentary tools in process of constructing some of the most monumental blocks of the social overhead capital. Such a policy would permit the community to confine the use of capitalistic methods to lines in which their advantages were too striking to be over-compensated by the cheapness of labor, or in which there were simply no alternatives outside of the highly capital-using range. As a result, the volume of investment needed to reduce unemployment by a given amount would be smaller than if the more capitalistic lines of the economy had to bear the major burden of the task. This, to be sure, was not denied by Preobrazhenski either. Suffice it to recall his remark that the intensification of agriculture might provide a way of tackling the problem of agricultural "disguised unemployment." Yet he was reluctant to move very far along this line of attack because he felt that this would require an undue reduction in industrial investment. Bazarov had no such qualms. Neither did Bukharin and Rykov who shared his ideas in this respect as well as in many others. For the contemporary student of economic development, this attitude will recall the "dual economy" strategy as reflected, for instance, in the Indian Second Five Year Plan, with its emphasis on highly capital-intensive development in steel, and on cottage production in textiles.*

(3) Bazarov's attitude toward technological change revealed the same judiciousness in approach. His statement that the new plants should be built on the basis of the most up-to-date methods left no doubt about his fervor for modernization. Bazarov wanted to modernize with discrimination, however. He realized that the new technological horizon offered a variety of alternatives; and he was opting for those which seemed most in line with the factor proportions prevailing in the Soviet economy. This was what made him so keen about the technological developments which might ultimately be capital-saving. Yet there were some rather formidable hurdles to be cleared from the path. Although electric power and the internal combustion engine made it possible to mechanize small-scale urban and agricultural production with smaller capital investments than the steam-based technology would have required, they would call for more capital (most certainly — in the construction stage) than the primitive nonmechanized technology they were about to replace. Furthermore, the new technological developments, while making the range of choices between different sizes of productive units more continuous, and thus making it possible to level up the bottom more easily, could certainly not do away with the advantages of "big-

* The logic of this policy was formulated very succinctly by Professor Eckaus: "Suppose that the respective demands for output are such that a large part of the available capital is drawn into the capital-intensive and fixed-coefficient sector. The amount of labor which can be absorbed in these sectors is dependent on the amount of capital available. Since capital is a scarce factor, labor employment opportunities in this sector are limited by its availability rather than by demand for output. The relatively plentiful supply is then pushed into the variable-coefficient sector and absorbed there as long as the marginal productivity of labor is higher than the wages it receives." ("The Factor Proportions Problem in Underdeveloped Areas," *American Economic Review*, 45 (September 1955), 559–560.)

ness." Indeed, the capital savings made possible by electrification and rationalization in the industrial field could not materialize until after the output in the individual plants or industries in question had reached a very large scale. Bazarov, it will be recalled, was most emphatic on the last point, and no doubt he was aware of the first. In a backward country, he insisted, simultaneous modernization in all areas of the economy would be a contradiction in terms. Such "superficial industrial expansion" would merely waste the available resources and skills by scattering them too thinly. The solution lay in using up the opportunities for major improvement in a definite sequence, with the largest industries and most developed regions heading the list. The willingness to settle for partial reconstruction of some of the old plants was certainly a part of the same strategy. But it was by no means the whole rest of it. In order to appraise fully Bazarov's approach, as well as the position of others, we must discard the implicit assumption of closed economy which underlay our discussion up to now, and reintroduce foreign trade into the picture.

◻

Soviet foreign economic relations, as will be recalled, played a role in the controversy right from the start, although the emphasis given to it by different participants varied markedly. If for the Bukharin of the early period the matter was of a secondary importance, this was undoubtedly due to his robust optimism about the potentialities of "unlocked turnover." To him foreign trade was merely an added, although valuable, stimulant to recovery; its main contribution consisted in the widening of the "internal market." Yet what seemed peripheral to Bukharin could not but appear in an altogether different light to less optimistic debaters who saw the threat to stability in the excess of the effective demand and not in the lack of it. Naturally most of them were in favor of foreign loans, with Preo-brazhenski being most emphatic in this respect. Moreover, while they were under no delusion as to the volume of credits that might be secured, they saw the possibilities of significant gains also in the plain and simple exchange of currently produced domestic goods against the foreign. Here, logically enough, it was Shanin and Sokol'nikov who tried hardest. The case for assigning high priority to investments in agriculture and in other lines with low capital intensity would now appear greatly strengthened. An economy adhering to such policies could receive via foreign trade the desired amounts of "capitalistic" goods at a smaller sacrifice of resources than if it had to produce them domestically. The infant industry cases were acknowledged, but treated as exceptions that confirmed the rule. Thus the back-breaking dilemma seemed happily resolved, and so were the specific issues encountered during the earlier discussion. The small size of the domestic capital-goods sector need not give cause for worry any more. Besides, the cumulative growth of agriculture would no longer have to entail a continuous drain on the capital-goods sector since its equipment would now be coming from abroad in response to the steadily growing exports of agricultural products.

Once again, the present-day Western reader would have little difficulty in discovering similarities between the position of the high officials of the Soviet *Narkomfin* and the views presented on a higher level of sophistication by reputable neoclassical economists. Yet one need not be very iconoclastic in order to recognize that the Soviet moderates were riding their comparative cost argument much too hard. They never raised the question of the appropriate degree of specialization and of its dependence on the behavior of physical returns, on the one hand, and of the world demand, on the other, and had nothing to say about the importance of the size of the exporting country with regard to the world market in this connection. They focused exclusively on capital/labor ratios without stopping to inquire about comparative endowments of other factors and of the nature of their relationship to the first two. Nor did they seem to notice that existence or nonexistence of agricultural overpopulation could make a good deal of difference in determining what the socially relevant comparative advantages actually were. Had such questions been merely posed, it would be impossible to deny that the Soviet Union of the midtwenties did not score well, from the Shanin-Sokol'nikov viewpoint, on any one of these counts. And while the most dramatic single development like the collapse of the world grain market was still in the incipient stage around 1925, the forces which had been pushing toward it since World War I were clearly in sight.

Yet the opponents of the "agriculture-first" policy did not make these points either (although Bazarov did touch upon one of them in a lighter vein by remarking that Shanin "presumably did not expect to import oil and coal"). Shanin's critics never earnestly attempted to come to grips with the line of thought which, if correct, would make their argument largely irrelevant. Instead, they simply bypassed it and proceeded on the basis of an implicit premise that while a measure of specialization and trade could by no means be a substitute for the vast investment effort in the nonagricultural sector, it would nevertheless represent an excellent device for achieving the desired results in a less resource-consuming way. To Bazarov the possibility of trading with the rest of the world was the indispensable corollary of his policy of selectivity and the careful timing of investment outlays. Increases in the supply of goods which did not have large domestic markets and could therefore not enjoy economies of scale were to come from imports rather than from the expansion of the domestic capacity. To Preobrazhenski and his friends whose preferences as between different areas of the economy were more skewed, foreign trade provided an opportunity to raise the supply of capital goods to Soviet industry well above the precarious levels which the domestic capacity for producing these goods would permit. It seemed equally clear to them that the priority assigned to the capital-goods industry could yield best results if comparative costs considerations were allowed to determine whether or not particular branches of this sector should be developed at home.

No doubt, in this case too the debate could not help leaving the Western reader with a sense of unfinished business. Some badly needed qualifications and elaborations were missing. Bazarov erred even from his own point of view when he argued that the first priority in the sphere of producers goods should go to "those types . . . the demand for which has already attained a sufficiently large level." He would have been more nearly right if he had added — "or was about to attain such a level." The ingenious stock-flow argument used by Preobrazhenski in order to emphasize the gains in speed of expansion of the capital-goods industry through foreign trade would have been improved if he had made clear that the most spectacular gain in supply in capital goods to be attained in this way would be in the nature of onceover increase, and could not be expected to continue in the long run.*

* Let us assume that the output of the community consists of capital goods K and consumers goods C, and that the desired increment of K can be either produced domestically (alternative I) or obtained via foreign trade by stepping up exports of C (alternative II). The advantages of the alternative II have been discussed in text. Here are the limitations:

(1) In the alternative II the addition to the domestic K-producing capacity would consist of the sum total of the annual inflows of K and (on assumption that K is self-reproducing) of their increments over the given period of time. In the alternative I the addition to capacity would be represented, after the time-lag equal to the construction period, by the K-producing stock which would then go on turning out the annual flow

Moreover, he was overstating the point when he suggested that if Russia of the twenties had been a capitalist country, she would have been certain to receive foreign loans large enough to make her development reasonably smooth. (It should not be assumed that by taking such a sanguine view of the efficacy of foreign investment under capitalism, Preobrazhenski was indulging in heresy. He was merely following the lead of Lenin who had argued a decade earlier that "the export of capital affects the development of capitalism in the countries to which it is exported tremendously accelerating it." [2]) Last but not least, the failure to meet the Shanin-Sokol'nikov challenge head-on was certainly regrettable. Still, as happened so often in this debate,

---

of K-goods. The net advantage of the alternative II (in terms of K-producing capacity) would be measured by the difference between the sum total of inflows of K and the size of the home-made K-producing stock; and while this difference could be taken to be positive, it would be obviously smaller after the completion of the home-made stock than prior to it. The alternative II could still appear preferable, particularly if the foreign production of K is more efficient than domestic production (which would be, to be sure, a standard case of comparative advantage). Yet the edge over the alternative I would now be smaller than it might appear at first sight.

(2) The cut in the domestic consumption of C which could secure additional inflows of foreign K via increased exports would be difficult to maintain in conditions of expanding economy and continuing shifts of population from the overpopulated agriculture to industry, particularly when income elasticity of demand for C is high. In order to keep the imports of K-goods on the previous level, the exports of C-goods would have to be provided for, to an increasing degree, by stepping up their output; and this would call for additions to the C-producing capital stock. The choice would now be between producing additional stocks of K-goods and additional stocks of C-goods; and while there might be perfectly good reasons for doing the latter rather than the former, the resulting gains would be of an entirely different order of magnitude than in the earlier case and would be once again based on comparative advantages in the conventional sense of the term.

(3) The last point is a familiar one. The notion that by stepping up the volume of our exports we could obtain a proportional increase in the volume of imports would be valid only under constant terms of trade — an assumption which may or may not hold, and if it does not, the whole picture would be certain to change sooner or later.

the case was better than the argument. But in order to appraise the contributions more fully, we must abandon still another restrictive assumption which has been adopted for expository purposes, and turn to the problem of long-range economic growth.

VIII

A Long-Range View

AMONG the many notable features of the debate not the least was the sketchy treatment accorded to the problem area which was ostensibly at its heart — long-range economic growth. Issues related to this matter were overshadowed by what Bazarov called "the worries of the day." As will appear, this was perhaps less odd than it might seem at first; but from the viewpoint of an outside observer attempting to get a rounded picture, and not prepared to take the basic premises for granted, this was not a very helpful procedure. To fill this gap would require a full-dress discussion of Marxian economic dynamics — a task obviously beyond the scope of this study. In the following sections, thus, the endeavor is rather to pull together those elements of long-range analysis which the debaters did introduce, and to consider to what extent some of the problems discussed in earlier chapters assume a different character as a result of the change in perspective.

□

Reference was made in the preceding chapter to two important backlogs confronting the Soviet economy of the twenties. While the debaters did not use the term "backlog," they were intensely aware of the underlying facts. The excitement about electrification and rationalization and the bitter complaints about the wretchedly low level of technology in wide areas of Soviet economy showed a clear realization of the high tension between actualities and potentialities, to borrow Professor Gerschenkron's phrase.[1] But while the doctrine which conditioned the debaters' thinking seemed to pull out all stops in extolling the advantages of large-scale production and the gains to be secured from technological progress, it was equally blunt in pointing out that these benefits could be had only at a heavy cost. As students of *Capital* were told in no uncertain terms, investment was an indispensable condition of long-range growth, and it had to be highly capital-intensive in order to be efficient. Furthermore, the net addition to capital stock was determined by the capacity of the capital-goods industries in relation to the capacity of the whole economy. This condition, formalized in the famous reproduction schemes of the second volume, was certainly severe on economies with a relatively small capital-goods sector at the starting point. Marx did not set up these schemes in order to devise an "optimum" rate of growth. He aimed, more modestly, at finding out which quantitative proportions between the major areas of the economy could allow for its continuous expansion on the basis of full-capacity output. His model showed that such a requirement could be equally well satisfied by several alternative combinations of relative sizes of capital-goods and consumers-goods sectors within the given total. Yet at the same time it did demonstrate that a higher ratio of the "Department I" to the "Department II" would result, other things being equal, in a higher rate of growth for the system as a whole. This clearly meant that in order to make an economy grow faster, the relative share of the capital-goods sector in the total output as well as in the total capital stock had to be raised above its previous level. And although the Marxian model taken by itself did not yield any policy recommendations one way or another, people whose minds were set on industrialization at the greatest possible speed could derive from the construct a powerful support for their contention that in order to secure a rapid and smooth advance in the future a discontinuous jump was needed now. They could claim that this conclusion was not inconsistent with the general tenor of the doctrine, in spite of the implicit and explicit warnings posted here and there.*

Naturally, therefore, it was Preobrazhenski who made especially extensive use of the model and of the supporting analysis. In his insistence on having investment-goods and consumer-goods industries arranged in a "marching combat order," and in his emphasis on the time-consuming nature of the gestation period of the new plant as well as in the accelerator-like notion of investment shooting ahead of the total output in cases of an upward shift in the rate of growth, he was closely following the Marxian line of thought. In some respects he could have extracted from the model a little more than he did. He could have proven in a rigorous way the point we have already touched upon during the discussion of Shanin's views: an economy A plowing back a larger portion of its investment into expansion of the capital-goods industry than an economy B would have its consumption show a lower rate of growth in the immediate future, but a higher rate of growth in the long run, because in the early period the comparative consumption levels would be dominated by the higher share of consumers-goods industries in the total investment of B and in later years by a growing difference between the volumes of total investment in A and B due to the faster expansion of the capital-goods industries in A. (The total national income of A could be assumed to grow faster right from the start, except for a brief initial period whenever the capital/output ratio in capital-goods

* E.g., "On the basis of social production, it must be ascertained, on what scale those operations which withdraw labor and means of production for a long time without furnishing in return any useful product, can be carried on without injuring those lines of production which do not only withdraw continually, or at several intervals, labor power and means of production, but also supply means of subsistence and of production" (*Capital*, II, p. 412). It was hardly surprising that Shanin quoted this passage in support of his plea for moderation.

industries would be much higher than in consumers-goods industry.* He did go both beyond *Capital* and beyond the call of necessity, however (although not more so than other prominent Marxists have done before him), when he declared that "the development of productive forces inevitably implies an increase in the relative share of the means of production [in total output]."[2] As a quick glance at the model in the second volume of *Capital* shows, the minimum condition for growth is fulfilled when the capacity of the investment-goods sector is in excess of the replacement needs of the whole system. Once the capacity of this sector had been raised to a level allowing for such an excess (with appropriate provision for increase in working population), the "development of productive forces" would be entirely compatible with the equiproportional increase of both sectors (in fact, even an edge in favor of consumers goods would be admissible as long as the margin over the replacement demand still existed). The reference to the technological progress being "as a rule" synonymous with the rise in organic composition of capital[3] helped matters only to a degree. Preobrazhenski was right when he pointed out that the models of the second volume failed to incorporate this funda-

---

* See G. A. Fel'dman, "K teorii tempov narodnogo dokhoda," *PKh* (November and December 1928). (For an illuminating discussion of Fel'dman's model, see E. D. Domar, *Essays in the Theory of Economic Growth* [New York, 1957], ch. ix.) The argument could then be turned around in order to demonstrate that an economy with the consumers-goods sector expanding faster than the investment-goods sector and with the capital/output ratio showing no decline, would, after the period of rapid growth, begin to level off and then to contract as soon as the replacement demand of the growing consumers-goods sector would absorb, and then exceed, the amount which the lagging capital-goods sector could produce over and above its own replacement needs. Actually, Preobrazhenski clearly hinted at this point when he argued, in a passage cited earlier, that reallocation of investment in favor of agriculture and against industry would affect unfavorably the over-all growth in the future, and he came even more closely to an explicit statement on the subject when he commented on one of his own arithmetical models (*VKA* XVIII [1927], p. 50); but not unlike many model builders before and after him, he failed to spell out his mathematics fully.

mental proposition of the Marxian theory.[4] But in order to make his point he would have had to demonstrate that this proposition was correct, and that an increase in capital per man was inevitably bound to involve an increase in capital per unit of output as well; and this he could not have proved even if he had tried. Bazarov did not make the last-mentioned distinction either; but he showed here, too, a better instinct than most of his colleagues when he refused to accept this particular "directive inequality" as a *sine qua non* of economic growth, and pointed out (although in a different context) that technological progress was not always capital-using.

Yet the practical importance of this exaggeration was not great. In a country attempting to raise its rate of economic growth with no significant idle capacity to fall back upon, the increase in the share of investment in the national income would be almost an arithmetical truism. It could be avoided only if this increase in the rate of growth were to involve a more than proportional expansion in the noncapitalistic sector or be paralleled by massive innovations of an immediate capital-saving effect — and no one, except for Shanin, ever suggested either of the two as a realistic possibility. On the whole, no doubt, Preobrazhenski went a considerable distance toward recasting Marxian schemes in an undogmatic fashion. He stiffened them quite properly by pointing out that the "constant capital" in a modern economy could not possibly wear out and be due for full replacement within one year — an amendment which clearly implied a much greater disparity between the increase of the gross investment and of the total output in cases of discontinuous growth than would follow from Marx' original equations.*

* True, such a departure from the original model would also imply a very substantial reduction in the ratio of replacement requirements to the gross national product. But this "gain" would be made spurious by the fact that the ratio of capital stock to the gross national product would be correspondingly higher.

At the same time, he introduced more flexibility into the picture by dropping the implicit assumptions of the constant capacity utilization and of the technologically fixed life-service period of the plant — conditions which, if literally obeyed, would rule out increases in output without prior investment in fixed capital, even as a short-run expedient. Moreover, as was shown repeatedly in the foregoing, he did not insist on aiming at the most advanced technology all the way down the line; and he admitted that the introduction of foreign trade into the picture would make a lot of difference. It would not be hard to show that such attempts at relaxation could claim sanction of the highest authority. Marx was fully aware of the first-approximation nature of his growth model; he explicitly admitted the possibility of capital-saving innovations in the third volume of *Capital;* and in a less well-known passage of *Theories of Surplus Value* he pointed out that a country which wanted to accumulate but had no capital-goods industry of its own, could help itself through the recourse to foreign trade.[5] But the participants of the Soviet debate have most certainly not arrived at these qualifications merely by having another look at the fine print.

The treatment of the second backlog provided another example of the putting of a time-honored tool to good use. To be sure, the bulk of the open as well as disguised unemployment in the Soviet economy of the twenties had its origin not in the displacement of labor by machine but in the mounting pressure of rural population against the limited area of cultivable land. Yet as eminent Western economists have pointed out recently,[6] it was precisely these conditions which made the Marxian-type unemployment plausible. With the capital stock too small to provide full employment on the basis of any available technology within the relevant range of choice, the introduction of labor-saving techniques would merely add to the existing pool of excess labor. The introduction of growth into the picture would point to a solution. The clash between considerations of efficiency and employment would be removed and the net social product of innovations would no longer be reduced by possible loss of income as a result of displacement, if the substitution of the new technology for the old were paralleled by an increase in the total volume of capital stock, which would more than compensate the reduction of labor requirements in modernized plants. To put it in more familiar terms, "deepening" had to be accompanied by "widening" in order not to make the reduction of one backlog lead to the perpetuation of the second. In pursuing this line of reasoning, the debaters led by Preobrazhenski were faithfully following Marx to whom the capacity-increasing effect of new investment was the only effective offset against the technological displacement. Here, once again, the model of the second volume would be on hand to remind us that a "combat-marching-order" arrangement of the two basic sections of the economy was called for in order to equip the unemployed with the necessary tools within a comparatively short span of time. Indeed, it was precisely this role of capital as the limiting factor which made the model fully applicable. Yet in this case, too, a stern classical proposition was softened by neo-classical amendments. Rapid addition to the stock of modern equipment was viewed as the most desirable way of eliminating unemployment in the long run. But to rely on it alone would mean clearly either having to wait a long time or having to run the risk of "superficial industrial expansion." Accordingly, a valiant attempt was made to split the difference, by directing one part of the investment toward projects which were bound to make possible a rapid growth of employment opportunities in the distant future, and by devoting the rest to the creation of capital-cheap and labor-absorbing facilities which could go into action much earlier. In addition, it was an advantage that some of the crucially important undertakings which were bound to be highly capital-intensive on the operation stage would permit a high degree of substitution of labor for capital on their construction stage. This would be, logically enough, exactly the same strategy which was shown a while ago to be appropriate with regard to the backlog in technology. To be sure, there was no unanimity as to the relative shares of the future-directed "big" and the present-oriented "small." Moreover, the way in which the balance was struck by the representatives of either view was highly intuitive and far from explicit, to say the least. But there was no attempt to deny the necessity of such a dual-economy approach as a pattern to be followed for a long time to come; and the most ardent "superindustrializers" did not aspire to anything like the proverbial "one-horse-to-one-nightingale" ratio in favor of the lines they wanted to develop.

Viewed against this background, the attitude toward the problem of long-run relationships between industry and agriculture falls into place, and the perfunctory way in which the matter was treated is easily explainable. Here was, to begin with, the most important single case of the "small" being put ahead of the "big." While the notion of superiority of the large-scale technology in the agricultural field appeared axiomatic, it was generally understood that there was still a wide range of opportunities for increases in the productivity of peasant farming which did not call for the introduction of bulky mechanized equipment. Consequently, the extensive application of highly "capitalistic" improvements was to be postponed until after the capital-goods industry which had to provide the physical ingredients for such retooling had been sufficiently expanded. This was what Preobraz-henski had in mind when he spoke of a "torrential flood" of capital which was to descend upon agriculture in the future. Similarly, it was recognized that industrial expansion would provide an important but not the only outlet for rural overpopulation, and that a part of the solution was to come from increasing the labor-absorbing capacity of agriculture, although opinions varied as to the relative importance of these two lines of attack. With regard to the future relationships between agriculture and other sectors, finally, the area of agreement was, if anything, even broader. All the debaters assumed that in a progressing economy industry was bound to grow faster than agriculture. Also to Shanin and Sokol'nikov their "agriculture-first" policy was nothing but a clever detour which would permit a speedier advance along the main highway later on. No attempt was made to sharpen this analysis by bringing in some equivalent of Engel's law, stressing a greater incidence of "growing points" in urban industry than in agriculture or commenting on Russia's factor endowments. It was apparently felt that Marxism in general, and the crusade of the first generation of its Russian adepts against the Populists in particular, had settled all these problems, once and for all, decades ago; and it was perhaps not accidental that the most systematic criticism of Shanin's position came from a non-Marxist and former Populist, Professor Nikolai Oganovski who argued, in a closely-reasoned paper, that agriculture, if deprived of a stimulant from outside, would lack a propelling force for continuous growth.[*] On the other hand, no one took exception when Bukharin spoke of dangers which stagnation or retrogression in agricultural field would have for the economy as a whole. In fact, Preobrazhenski almost gave him one better by coining the formula: "take more from a still larger income than under

[*] In areas with abundant land, he stressed, peasant farming, left to itself, would level off after reaching a certain level of "peasant satiety," while in densely populated areas there would be a clearcut downward trend, with progressing fragmentation of land as its main vehicle. "*Stagnation* or retrogression — these are inevitable consequences of the 'self-sustained' development of agriculture without a parallel and more rapid development of industry which creates, in the first place, a market for the products of agriculture" (Promyshlennost' i sel'skoe khozyaistvo," in *Promyshlennost' i narodnoe khozyaistvo* [Moscow, 1927], pp. 203–204.)

capitalism." It was the problem of the once-over "hump" of forced saving in the transition period from "restoration" to "reconstruction," and not the long-range perspective that divided the spirits.

□

Such were, in broadest outline, the major building blocks which the debaters of the twenties borrowed from the Marxian storeroom in their discussion of long-range problems. It is not difficult for the Western-trained economists to recognize familiar ideas in spite of somewhat outlandish garb; and it can be shown easily that some of the points, if pursued a bit further, gain in sharpness and throw additional light on the argument of the preceding chapters:

(1) The dimensions of technological backlog are clearly affected by the shift in perspective. All modifications in conventional approach, shown to be necessary in case of a temporary interruption of growth would apply *a fortiori* with regard to an economy which happened to be backward also prior to the interruption. Such an economy would be facing, at least in some of its major areas, a host of technological alternatives which had originated in response to entirely different factor endowments but which succeeded in acquiring a clear superiority well beyond the range of the specific scarcity relationships that triggered them off.* This

---

* It could be pointed out that some of these new methods would represent (following the distinction introduced by Professor Hicks in his *Theory of Wages*) "autonomous" rather than "induced" innovations, hence they need not, theoretically speaking, exhibit a "capitalistic" bias, and to that extent the investment requirements involved in their application would be smaller than in case of capital-using technological change. Yet at the same time most of the capital-saving innovations of our days involve a cheapening of large-size equipment rather than a rise in the comparative efficiency of small-size equipment because it is the large size sector of the economy which provides the best facilities for producing a steady flow of *all* kinds of inventions, and because economies of scale are among important sources of savings on capital costs. Consequently, a backward economy in this case, too, would be faced with technological alternatives involving, by and

superiority, it goes without saying, would be the more striking, the longer the time which the method in question had
at its disposal in order to overcome the tribulations of its
early trial-and-error stage, and to surround itself with a
cluster of adequate technologies and capacity sizes in the
complementary lines: Professor Dahmen's[7] "developmental
blocks" constitute a particularly pronounced case of this kind.
Yet this very maturity of the newer methods which would
strongly enhance their attractiveness would make it highly
advantageous (and, in some instances, imperative) to have
the technological borrowing done in single packages whose
size would tend to be large in relation to the total capacity
of an underdeveloped economy.

(2) It may be objected that the above statement, at best,
tells only one half of the story. While the advantages of the
up-to-date methods are great, the marginal time preference
in such a backward economy is high, and this can effectively
limit the adoption of up-to-date methods. True enough; yet
even from the viewpoint of fairly conventional assumptions
the force of this objection can be softened in the case under
consideration. To begin with, the central authority in a
controlled economy can substitute its own time-preference
for that of the population and set the (actual or virtual)
rate of interest accordingly. Moreover, as was pointed out
repeatedly in recent Western writings,[8] in an economy
which would be adding at a high rate to its capital stock
over a long time to come, the future rate of interest could
be assumed to decline faster than in an economy with a
slower rate of capital accumulation; and anticipation of
such trend would act as a stimulus to make investments into
durable structures follow the technological pattern which

---

large, higher capital/labor ratios and higher minima of capital outlays than
it had until then; and the fact that the cost of modern equipment had been
reduced by innovation, would enhance this equipment's ability to compete
aggressively against the less mechanized technology.

would be, as it were, a step ahead of the present factor proportions. True, the persistence of Marxian-type unemployment would tend to weaken the force of this stimulus; but such an offset would operate primarily against lines which would, owing to their relatively low capital/output ratio, show little sensitivity to prospective changes in the rate of interest.

In other words, the introduction of growth into the picture gives a different slant to the problem of choice of priorities. But this influence operates through the anticipation not only of changes in relative factor supplies but of developments on the demand side as well. Modern producers-goods industries which entail substantial economies of scale find themselves in a heavy predicament in an economy adding to its capital stock at a low annual rate or having too small a total stock to generate a sizeable replacement demand. In such conditions, it might be indeed a better part of wisdom to settle for a smaller (if less efficient) size of the producing unit or to rely on imports.* But the anticipation of a steady and rapid increase in the demand for additional plant would tilt the scales the other way — particularly since the growth of domestic demand for the assets in question could be now assumed (barring a happy coincidental change abroad) to

* It might be objected that economies of scale often could be achieved within the limits of a single plant and that situations in which the capacity of such a single plant would be too large to satisfy the total domestic demand for the durable good in question would be quite rare, except for very small or very poor countries. True, but (1) some external intraindustrial economies might be of importance (repair work, supply of spare parts, pools of skilled labor, not to speak of massive pieces of social overheads); (2) given a certain number of already existing plants whose size had been determined in the past by a lower demand for the good in question and, probably also by an inferior technology, it might not be warranted to scrap them and to build better and larger plants (or to add the latter to the former) unless a pronounced and enduring increase in demand would be anticipated. The validity of the point made in the text does not rest on the assumption that the advantages of scale of the different kinds mentioned above are ubiquitous; it is sufficient to establish that they are not exceptional in order to feel that a change in the rate of growth is bound to make a difference.

grow more rapidly than the world's demand for the exports of the economy in question. Except for the last-mentioned point, the same holds true with regard to large lumps of social overhead capital. The construction of these items entails a risk of monumental waste and might therefore not materialize unless the construction of units using their services was definitely expected to follow suit and to develop on a large scale. On the other hand, to be sure, the completion of such a chunk of "external economies" might spell the difference between an adequate and less-than-adequate inducement to invest in the complementary productive facilities — a second part of the same argument which received rather more attention in the recent writings than the first. (Bazarov, it may be recalled, was equally explicit about both of them.)

(3) Yet while the process of growth would be self-reinforcing right from the start, the actual pay-off would set in as newer and better plants started to emerge. For quite a while the economy would be doubly blessed. On the one hand, the social cost of expanding could be greatly reduced; this would be due both to the greater ease of enforcing a high rate of saving at higher levels of per-capita income and to an enlarged physical capacity to grow. At the same time, the opportunities for growth, with backlogs in technology and reserves of unemployed manpower acting as offsets to diminishing returns and with the not unlikely benefits of scale on the all-economy level, could be assumed to persist for a more or less protracted period of time. The interplay of Lerner's marginal efficiency of investment and marginal productivity of capital which we already saw at work in another context; the external economies in Pigovian and in Rosenstein-Rodan-Scitovsky sense; Hayek's "investment that increases demand for capital" — all these familiar concepts apply in such a situation. And all of them seem to favor overwhelmingly the daring over the timid.

(4) In view of such breath-taking prospects it may seem odd that the most ardent proponents of rapid growth deemed it necessary to rely so heavily on arguments based on short-term considerations. Actually, the paradox was apparent rather than real because the two approaches supplemented each other. Without a perspective of rapid long-range growth, goods famine and arrears in replacement are very weak reeds upon which to lean. With regard to excess demand, Shanin's argument in favor of cuts in investment was logical, to say the least. And to invest in an expansion of the capital-goods industries in a poor country merely in order to meet the pent-up replacement demand seems almost frivolous since such demand could not by definition be expected to last for long. But the risk of excess capacity would not arise if the economic expansion was known to be continuing full-blast well after the accumulated loss in capital had been made good. Besides, it is obviously easier to contain inflationary pressures when there is a larger total capital stock than a smaller one, even if the increased volume of consumers goods would now represent a lower share of the social output. Yet not merely do long-range considerations bolster the short-term argument; the same was true the other way round. By pointing out that not only the ceiling but also the floor of investment was high, a distinct "or-else" connotation was introduced. It was possible to argue, in effect, that a certain "critical minimum" of investment effort exists: the arrears of replacement would perform the same functions as the rapid population growth in some recent discussions of economic development in backward areas. Moreover, a slow development in conditions of the rampant shortage of goods would do little to remove the economy from the neighborhood of the "inflation barrier," and this would make for a highly unstable equilibrium. In brief, a note of urgency, added to the plea for speed, would be a most valuable support because despite everything said in the

preceding paragraphs, a slower pattern of growth still had its attractions. And this leads us straight to the final point.

(5) To be sure, the cheerful conclusion that expansion feeds on itself fails to do full justice not only to the facts but also to the arguments of the leading debaters. As has been shown time and time again, all of them knew that the process of accelerated growth could be self-reinforcing in a much more ominous sense when pushed recklessly along the path of "building factories with future bricks" or pursued in supine disregard of the possibilities of a peasant strike — and it was obviously the early stages which offered the greatest opportunities for getting off the tracks. More generally, an economy trying to step up its rate of growth, by definition, exposes its physical capacity and its saving potential to much stronger pressures than they are adapted to. Consequently, everything that has been said previously about the necessity of sharp discrimination in uses of scarce capital would apply here with redoubled force. Since some of the most capital-using areas would now be strongly favored, it would be absolutely indispensable to cut down on the application of capital in uses allowing for a greater elasticity of substitution — the "dual economy" policy would carry in such a situation the sanction of the neoclassical orthodoxy. For the same reasons, the importance of the foreign trade would become strikingly evident; the more pronounced were the prospective gains of large-scale development in some lines, the more pressing would be the necessity for relying on imports in areas not equally affected by the shift in comparative advantages. Also the possibilities of gaining speed by building up some of the needed capital stocks on the basis of imports, finally, now would represent a greater asset to the economy than in periods of smooth development.

The ingenuity which Bazarov and Bukharin of post-1926 vintage showed in exploring such possibilities of relaxation is impressive. It is equally remarkable that the extremist Preobrazhenski did not attempt to play them down or to rule out their use. Yet none of them ever attempted to round out the picture by inserting a massive point of fact, presumably because they took it for granted; only Stalin, never reluctant to emphasize the obvious, touched on it briefly when he spoke of the Russian industry as the "most large-scale in the world." Indeed, even after all the necessary qualifications were introduced into the original Marxian scheme and after the indivisibility-cum-complementarity assumption was trimmed down to size, the situation still remained grim. A backward country starting "from scratch" with no substantial assistance from outside (or spectacularly good terms of trade) would find it difficult to stomach a "dual economy" policy of the kind envisaged by Bazarov and Bukharin, not to speak of Preobrazhenski's stronger medicine. But the Soviet Union of the twenties, in spite of its age-old comparative backwardness and of the beating it took during the Civil War, was definitely not such kind of a country. It had inherited from the prerevolutionary regime an industrial sector which had been growing since the mideighties at a rate comparing quite favorably with some of the advanced Western countries. It had a sizeable nucleus of capital-goods production which had been expanding much faster than the industry as a whole, and which accounted for nearly two-thirds of the gross turnover of the Russian large-scale industry in 1913;[9] more particularly, its ferrous metallurgy was turning out in that year roughly around 4 million tons in each of its three major subgroups (pig iron, crude steel, and rolled steel) and showed, in its youngest and largest southern branch, a pronounced technological superiority over its British and German opposite numbers.[10] In addition, the last three decades before the revolution witnessed a powerful drive for the expansion of the railroads which continued well into the first war years, and which represented a typical case of building ahead of demand; a pause, or at least a slackening in this expansion would have released substantial resources of the Russian heavy industries for construction of plant in other lines. The machine-building and metal-working industries, finally, which had been the weakest spot in the capital-goods sector prior to 1913 experienced rapid growth under the spur of armament demand during the three years that followed.

The significance of the coexistence of these massive blocks of modern technology and vast areas of primeval backwardness was repeatedly stressed in the Soviet literature as a key to the solution of the paradox of socialist victory in a nonindustrialized country. Lenin put it quite crisply in a note jotted down on the margins of his copy of Bukharin's *Ekonomika perekhodnogo perioda:* "without a certain level of capitalist development, we would get nowhere." [11] Indeed; and this was the missing, but crucially important, link in the economic argument as well. The "dual economy" did not have to be created from scratch, and the community attempting to rearrange its resources could be spared the initial build-up of some of the most capital-using components of the Marxian "Department I" as well as of some of the bulkiest "external economies." The tension between actualities and potentialities was there, but reduced to dimensions at which it was, with all relaxation devices playing their part, a stimulus rather than an invitation to choose between stagnation and explosion. And by the same token what would have otherwise appeared as caution would now seem like a failure of nerve. Foregoing a full-dress initial investment in a line which could be expected to have a large market in the not-too-distant future was one thing. It was quite a different matter to whittle down an already existing capital stock bit by bit while realizing that its full services would be needed again before long, and that as a result of contraction precious treasure of skills and scientific know-how would be dissipated and opportunities for gradual cumulative im-

provement thrown away; Bazarov was everlastingly right
when he pointed this out against Shanin. An expansion path
which would be bold and realistic as well, seemed within
the realm of the possible.

IX

The Final Decision

Our survey of the Soviet industrialization controversy has shown that toward the end of the great debate the two main groups were much closer to each other than at its beginning: Bukharin and his followers admitted explicitly the inevitability of discontinuous growth, while Preobrazhenski became increasingly outspoken about the risks involved in such policy. It would not be unnatural to expect, under such circumstances, an attempt to work toward some middle ground.

Actual developments did not follow this path. The resolutions on economic policy adopted by the Fifteenth Congress of the CPSU could indeed be interpreted as a step toward a synthesis between the older right-wing and left-wing conceptions. However, this change of attitude had its corollary not in a rapprochement between the majority and the opposition, but in the crushing of the latter by force. All the leaders of the left wing, including Trotsky and Preobrazhenski, were expelled from the party. But this turn of events, however stunning, paled into insignificance in comparison with what came later. The "synthesis" went overboard within less than two years, and the new policy line which superseded it swung to extremes which the most ardent "super-industrializers" of the suppressed left wing had never imagined. The First Five Year Plan proclaimed as its objective an expansion in investment goods-output to the level which would make the fixed capital of the economy double within five years — a rate of growth unparalled in history. And while according to the professed intentions this expansion was to be accompanied by a marked increase in per capita consumption, in the process of actual fulfillment the first part of the program was pushed through unwaveringly at the expense of the second. What was the reason for this bizarre zigzag course? What were the motives which made the Soviet leadership embark upon a policy about the dangers of which there had seemed to be practical unanimity?

◘

One of the conceivable lines along which the answer might be sought follows to its logical extreme the trail blazed by Preobrazhenski. Boiled down to essentials, it consists in pointing out that the Soviet economy toward the end of the twenties had faced a choice between stagnation on the existing intolerably low level (if not an actual contraction below it) or expansion at a very rapid pace, and that the full portent of this "either-or" was not recognized until the policies based on more sanguine expectations had been disproved by the facts. However, such an hypothesis, in spite of some *prima facie* plausibility, is not borne out by the results of our discussion. True, our account of the debate uncovered several factors which could be considered as conducive to sharp discontinuities in growth: large arrears in replacement, indivisibility-cum-complementarity phenomena, and high capital/output ratio causing the investment to be the multiple of the normal output flow it is supposed to produce. But all these factors, it will be recalled, offered relaxation possibilities. Some of the overdue replacements could be postponed further more easily than others, either because the contribution of the equipment in question was of lesser significance or because of the greater durability of this equipment and the greater possibility of extending its service-life by relatively minor additional outlays. In certain areas expansion was possible without large amounts of indivisible equipment, and in some of them output increases could be used, *via* foreign trade, to obtain large quantities of such equipment from abroad. This would lessen the need for "advancing along the broad front" and permit dispensing, up to a point, with the building-up of new stocks in order to obtain the desired flows. In the case of very significant indivisibilities, finally, there was the possibility of easing the burden through tackling them one by one.

No doubt, even with all these devices used to the hilt, it was still true that in the case under consideration the further rise in output would hit capacity limits and consequently would require a steep increase in investment — a point on which everybody agreed by 1927. But it would be rash to conclude that, for a country with a sizeable nucleus of modern industry and of social overhead, the only way to avoid a "downward spiral" and to secure a continuous expansion would be to double the existing capital stock within five years. The advocates of rapid industrialization were certainly wise in refraining from such extravagant assertions. But it would have been, if anything, even more fantastic for them as well as for their fellow debaters to go to the opposite extreme and to have taken seriously the idea that the capacity of the capital-goods industries at the disposal of Soviet planners and the proficiency of the Soviet construction work would permit not only the doubling of the capital stock of the industry within half a decade but, in addition, the raising of the output of consumers goods by 70 per cent during the same period. Everything they had been saying about the Soviet situation and about the mechanics of the Marxian model of the "expanded reproduction" flagrantly contradicted this central proposition of the First Five Year Plan.*

---

* It is therefore somewhat astonishing that Professor Dobb, writing nearly two decades later, seemed to take the targets of the First Five Year Plan quite seriously. The astonishment is compounded by the fact that at the same time he tried (albeit rather cautiously) to make use of the "indivisi-

Another and more widely accepted line of explanation points to the need to strengthen the military potential of the country due to the turn for the worse in the international situation. As has been pointed out more than once, considerations of preparedness have played an important role in the discussion from the very beginning, with all participants without exception making more or less generous allowance for them. However, in the form in which the argument is usually presented, it tends to raise more questions than it answers. It is undoubtedly true that since the end of 1927 the tenor of official pronouncements has reflected the concern about rising international tension. Yet it is hard to believe that the breaking-off of diplomatic relationships by the British Conservative government, the assassination of the Soviet Ambassador in Warsaw by an *émigré* terrorist or Chiang Kai-shek's turning the tables on his Communist allies, disturbing as these events undoubtedly were, could be interpreted as a prelude to an armed intervention. Furthermore, if Stalin's repeated warnings about the greatly increased danger of war were to be taken literally, the policy

---

bility" argument in order to stress the gravity of decisions the Soviet planners were facing. (*Soviet Economic Development since 1917* [New York, 1948], pp. 4–5, 235–237). This looks indeed like trying to have it both ways — "eat one's cake and having it too," on the one hand, dramatic "either/or," on the other. Also the introduction of the rural overpopulation into the picture (pp. 23–24) does not improve the argument, even if the assumption that the total output of food will not be reduced as a result of migration to the cities is unreservedly accepted. Given the high rate of expansion envisaged by the First Five Year Plan and the highly capital-intensive nature of the industries which were allotted top priorities by the investment program, the massive shift of the rural surplus population to the cities could help to meet the planned targets only if paralleled by a drastic increase in the supply of heavy industrial equipment for the new members of the labor force. Such an increase, in turn, would call for a sharp switch of domestic capital-goods industries toward producing such equipment at the expense of equipment for consumers-goods industries and/or for a steep rise in imports of foreign machinery which could come about (owing to virtual absence of foreign lending) only as a result of a correspondingly pronounced rise in exports of primary products. In either case, a decline in domestic consumption would be inevitable. With regard to exports, incidentally, Professor Dobb admits this quite explicitly.

of the First Five Year Plan would look very much like a suicide prompted by a fear of death. If the Soviet Union had been attacked at any time between 1929 and 1932, it would have faced all the disadvantages of rapid growth with practically none of its advantages; the large-scale output of armaments was still a long way off, and, in the meantime, the country was in the throes of the deepest social and economic upheaval it had seen since the Civil War. Even if the men who were responsible for the final decisions did not anticipate the full extent of the crisis their policy was to cause, they must have been aware that the risks were grave. Stalin's earlier statements about the dangers of breaking with the peasants leave no doubt on this score. Indeed, all the unquestionable benefits from the viewpoint of preparedness which the "general line" did bring about were due to the fact that the real danger of war did not arise until after Hitler's seizure of power in 1933 — and the actual attack did not materialize until eight years later.

Did not the adopted policy, nevertheless, turn out to be (in retrospect, at least) the only correct one? It would be rash to assume that a reduced but still significant rate of industrial growth could not have resulted in a sizeable increase in the Soviet military potential between 1928 and 1941. The difference between the two patterns in terms of the output of armament goods no doubt would have been considerable.* But the higher over-all efficiency in the economic system and stronger social cohesion might have gone

* This difference, it might be added, would be substantially greater than what would follow from the mere comparisons of the total national incomes under both alternative patterns. An economy with a smaller rate of growth would show, other things being equal, not only a lower national income but also a smaller share of investment in this income. Furthermore, the part of the total investment devoted to the expansion of the basic capacity would be here smaller than in the alternative case. Consequently, an attempt to have the same share of armaments in national income would involve, for an economy with a slower rate of growth, a proportionally much greater cut in the expansion of the basic capacity and possibly even its actual shrinkage. If the aim of the operation is to reach the peak arma-

a long way toward compensating for this difference, particularly if the country were, as a result, spared the destruction of the flower of its military leadership. Besides, there is ample room for speculation as to what the whole course of events might have been if the powerful German Communist party had been allowed to practice, in the decisive years 1930–1933, the policy of the popular front (which was to become the stock-in-trade of the Comintern a few years later), instead of directing its heaviest attacks against the tottering Weimar Republic. No doubt, any alternative decision would have involved risks — but risks of a different extent, different incidence in time, and, last but not least, of a different kind. Some of them could not possibly have been visualized by 1928, but others very definitely might. Why did the Soviet leadership decide in favor of one set of these risks rather than of another? In order to answer, it is necessary to turn from these general observations on discontinuities in the process of growth or on trends in international politics in the late twenties to a somewhat more pedestrian subject. We have in mind the events which took place in the Soviet economy during the interval between the Fifteenth Congress and the launching of the First Five Year Plan.

□

The beginning of 1928 saw large consignments of leftist "superindustrializers" move toward faraway places of exile.

---

ment output at one jump, and if the war is not expected to last very long, this is not too bad. The need for the whole operation may end before the shrinkage of the basic industrial capacity will begin to affect adversely the armament output. But if the estimated peak of the armament program is so high that it can be attained only gradually, and if the war is expected to last a long time, a policy is needed which will permit making the first installment of armaments sufficiently great, and at the same time to increase the basic capacity sufficiently, to build up the armament potential through time over and above its (appallingly large) replacement needs, as well as to secure some minimum of civilian requirements without which the whole economy would begin to disintegrate.

But at the same time their dire predictions were coming true. By January the amount of grain collected by the state purchasing agencies was roughly one-third less than in the same period of the preceding year. During the following months it rose only to drop again in the spring; and the methods of reprisals and forcible confiscations which were largely responsible for this temporary increase stirred up again the feelings of bitterness and resistance which had been dormant during the seven years of the NEP. The goods famine of 1925 repeated itself on a much greater scale, and there could be no longer any doubt about its meaning; the Soviet peasant was willing and able to bolt at the attempts to make him give up more in exchange for less.

The reaction of the leading representatives of two major groupings to the new developments was consistent with their attitudes in the preceding period. Preobrazhenski, in a clandestinely circulated document, interpreted the grain collection crisis as a striking confirmation of his analysis and conclusive proof that the official policy had failed. Yet while he approved of stern action against what he termed the kulak offensive, he was outspoken in stressing that if poor peasants will step up their output at the expense of kulaks, such an increase will be largely absorbed by their own consumption and will make only a small contribution to the marketable surplus. As a result, new emergency measures will be needed; and this "will make the sturdy middle peasant languish economically (*zastavit khozyaistvenno zaskuchat' krepkogo serednyaka*) and may cause a more dangerous reduction in sowings on the part of this stratum. . . . We can obtain grain from these strata [i.e., poor and middle peasants] only by using economic means, only via exchange of commodities, and we have to use economic means also in order to achieve a reduction of consumption of agricultural products in the villages by increasing demand for industrial consumers goods. This, however, calls for a definite tempo of increase in industrial production." [1] (In this connection, incidentally, he voiced the hope that American capitalists might be more willing than their weaker and less self-confident European brethren to extend long-term credit to the Soviet Union.) Bukharin and Rykov, as one might expect, issued grave warnings about the policy of reprisals and forcible seizure of grain (they were to speak of the "military feudal exploitation of the peasantry" a year later.) And they stressed with redoubled force the importance of pecuniary incentives for increases in peasant output and savings as well as the need for larger investment assistance to agriculture. Some of their strong statements quoted in earlier chapters were made in these troubled months. Within this general framework, they seemed to favor such stopgap measures as an increase in the price of grain or (should this prove ineffective) the import of grain, preferably on a credit basis, but, if need be, also at the price of diverting some scarce foreign currency from the purchase of capital goods.* They apparently assumed that in the meantime the improvement in peasant confidence would result in an increase of agricultural output followed by a less than proportional increase in peasant demand, and that recent investments in industry as well as steps toward further increase in capacity utilization would begin to bear fruit before long.

It was at this juncture that Stalin parted company with his allies and stole a march on his left-wing opponents. He did not question the diagnosis of the situation given by others. Indeed, amid fulminations against kulak "sabotage" he admitted that the shortage of industrial goods on the

---

* We say, "they seemed," because the recommendations mentioned above are taken not from the enunciations of the two men but from Stalin's blistering attack on them in April 1929 (*Sochineniya*, XII, p. 63). Also the phrase about "military feudal exploitation" is cited there. In spite of the source of information being less than unimpeachable it is quite likely that Bukharin and Rykov actually defended such views, particularly since policy measures along these lines had been actually applied, if to a moderate extent, during 1928.

peasant market, aggravated by an increase in the peasant earnings as a result of a good harvest, had hit not only the kulaks but the bulk of the peasantry, and made all of them strike back by cutting deliveries.[2] (He could have added that also the policy of keeping the procurement prices of grain stable in the face of rising demand did not make the peasants very eager to deliver.) He was more forthright than ever before in stressing the relation between the goods famine and the changes in investment policy;[*] and as late as 1929 he still kept insisting that the possibilities of improvement in efficiency within the framework of small-scale peasant farming were far from exhausted.[3] His substantive criticism of the policy proposals of the Bukharin-Rykov faction, finally, did not go beyond pointing to some very obvious difficulties which the authors of these proposals would certainly be the last to deny: Stalin stressed that the increase in grain prices would have unfavorable effects on real wages and that imports of food might develop at the expense of imports of industrial equipment.[4] He qualified the last point by admitting that the Soviet government was getting through various channels, offers of foreign credits for the purchase of grain; yet he defended the decision to turn down these offers by arguing that their purpose consisted in testing the stamina of the Soviet regime. Bukharin and Rykov favored acceptance.

But Stalin revealed very clearly the deeper motives which underlay his change of mind when he asked, in his characteristic style: "What is meant by not hindering kulak farming? It means setting the kulak free. And what is meant by setting

---

[*] "Industrial reconstruction means the transfer of resources from the field of the production of articles of consumption to the field of the production of means of production . . . But what does it mean? It means that money is being invested in the construction of new enterprises, that the number of new towns and new consumers is increasing while, on the other hand, the new enterprises will begin to turn out additional masses of commodities only in three or four years' time. It is obvious that this does not help to overcome the goods famine." (*Ibid.*, p. 267.)

the kulak free? It means giving him power." [5] On the face of it, this looked like a fairly weak syllogism even by its author's usual standards. There was nothing either in the logic of things or in the tenets of accepted doctrine to warrant the view that the policy advocated by Bukharin and Rykov would inevitably result in "giving power to the kulaks" and in the restoration of capitalism. In fact, Stalin did not seem to believe this two years earlier when he had declared, with a long supporting quotation from Lenin, that only defeatists could see a danger in the growth of "small private capital" in the villages because this growth "is being compensated and overcompensated by such decisive facts as the development of our industry which strengthens the position of the proletariat and of the socialist forms of the economy." [6] Yet he was obviously speaking now in deadly seriousness, and what was vastly more important, the consistent application of the Bukharin-Rykov recipe was undoubtedly fraught with the gravest political dangers. To have a fairly rapid industrialization sustained, to a considerable extent (although, of course, not exclusively) by the peasants' readiness to expand their sales faster than their purchases was, theoretically speaking, a possibility, particularly when backed up by sharp selectivity in the allocation of scarce capital resources and by the proper use of vast reserves of idle manpower. Yet the macroeconomic equilibrium attained in such a way would be exceedingly tenuous and exposed to rude jolts — the crisis of grain collections proved this beyond the possibility of a doubt. In order to maintain the precarious balance at such sharp turnings in the road, the regime would have to combine measures of direct control with additional inducements. But the well-to-do peasants, with the days of War Communism still fresh in their memory, could be relied upon to resist the first and spurn the second. In such a situation, it might not have been possible to avoid exploring a new line of approach and attempting to earn the good will of the upper strata of the peasantry by opening up for them avenues of political influence even if confined, at first, to the level of local government. In fact, as Stalin grimly noted, demands of such kind were already voiced, albeit timidly, on the periphery of the party.[7] Such attempts, however, would most definitely have evoked a bitter resistance on the part of the radical elements in the working class and of the young intelligentsia which had felt frustrated and repelled by the NEP "normalcy." As a result, the system of authoritarian dictatorship would have become increasingly shot through by elements of political pluralism and quasi-democratic pressure politics. The ruling party while nominally monolithic would have tended to become an arena for the bitter clashes of organized factions reflecting in one way or another the pushes and pulls which would come from the most articulate groups in the society. Such a state of things certainly did not look like a remote possibility in view of the intraparty feuds of the twenties; and the vacillating attitude which was shown, according to Stalin,[8] by the lower echelons of the party hierarchy and governmental apparatus during the critical months of 1928, underlined the gravity of the situation.

The conclusions were obvious. A policy of moderate tempos which would strengthen the position of the upper strata of the villages and would make the adroit balancing between them and the unruly radicals of the cities a necessity could be adopted only as a temporary expedient. Had such a course been pursued over a long period of time, the regime would have stood to lose not only from its possible failures but also from its successes. The alternative to such retreats and maneuvers leading to the gradual erosion of the dictatorial system was clearly a massive counterattack which would have broken once and for all the peasants' veto power over the basic decisions on economic policy. A high speed industrialization with a strong emphasis on the capital-goods sector which Stalin now favored provided the logical line for such a counterattack; and here the risk constellation would have been entirely different. The success of such an alternative would have been an unqualified triumph. The economic potential of the country would have risen to a level at which further vigorous expansion in productive capacity would no longer have been incompatible with an increase in consumption standards strong enough to keep inflationary pressures at bay. The frontiers of the state-controlled sector of the economy would have expanded tremendously at the expense of the individualist peasant agriculture and would have continued to expand in the wake of high-powered capital accumulation while the steady increase in industrial output would sap the roots of the peasant resistance and make agriculture more dependent in its day-to-day operation on supplies of city goods. But was not such a perspective utterly fantastic in view of everything that has been said thus far? Could not the multiplier effect of the rapidly-expanding investment volume in a backward economy be relied upon to throw the whole system out of gear and to set off a political explosion before the capacity-increasing effect of this investment had smoothed the waves?

□

The experience of the First Five Year Plan provides an answer to this question. It is not our task to set out in any detail the trial-and-error process by which the answer was arrived at. It is sufficient to state in the barest outline the main results. The disturbances which all the participants in the debate had expected from the much milder forms of the "shift of means of production toward producing means of production" did not fail to assert themselves with a vengeance. The glaring discrepancy between the targets set and the normal capacity of the existing plants called for a large-scale influx of additional labor and pushed the utilization of available equipment deep into the range of increasing costs, thus extending to an unheard-of degree the divergence between the increase in consumable output and in the labor force. Simultaneously, the new plant which could bring relief was at many crucial points slowed down in its completion, or limited in its operation, by bottlenecks in those complementary lines in which such shotgun adjustments between labor and equipment had proved even less workable than elsewhere; the solemn injunctions of the Fifteenth Congress about shortening the duration of the construction period were swept away. The ensuing drastic cut in consumption levels evoked a resistance which reached its peak in the open economic warfare of the villages against the government during the early thirties and which survived in a subdued form as a downward pressure on the productivity of agricultural and industrial labor. And there was, finally, the blunt fact that in a period of rapid industrialization even the most powerful government cannot afford to prevent money wages from rising. But the prophecies of doom did not come true because of the landslide-like change in the institutional framework which all the participants in the industrialization debate had assumed would last for decades and which provided a basis for their theoretical constructions. The supression of the limited independence of the trade unions ended the possibility of organized opposition against the catastrophic fall in real wages. An important "barrier to the tempo of the socialist accumulation" was thus effectively disposed of. The most momentous upheaval, however, consisted in the fact that the new device which Stalin first announced at the end of 1927 and which became increasingly crucial to him as the crisis deepened went to work full blast. The wholesale collectivization of agriculture did away with the peasants' "freedom to choose the time and the terms at which to dispose of their surpluses." It was now up to the state to set these terms and thus to determine the rate of peasant saving.

Preobrazhenski was undoubtedly right when he exclaimed in his self-castigating speech several years later: "Collectivization — this is the crux of the matter! Did I have this prognosis of the collectivization? I did not." [9] He was careful not to add that neither did Stalin at the time when the industrialization debate was in full swing. And he was wise not to point out that the decision to collectivize hinged not on superior intellectual perspicacity but on the incomparably higher degree of resolve to crush the opponent with utter disregard of the staggering human costs of the operation.

To be sure, the initial fee for the use of the new-fangled tool was appallingly high. The unwillingness of the peasants to accept the worsened terms of trade was dramatically intensified by their revolt against the loss of status, and expressed itself, among others, in the wholesale slaughter of livestock. In order to make up for this decline in draft power and to weld the newly-created collective farms into workable units, it was imperative to press forward large-scale mechanization of agriculture simultaneously with the re-equipment of basic industry instead of letting the first follow the second. The tremendous increase of capital requirements implied in such a decision could not but accentuate general tension and make the reduction in consumption levels still more severe. But at the same time powerful weapons to deal with these difficulties were provided. By assuming direct command over the whole economy and by backing it with the application of outright compulsion and repression on an unparalleled scale, the system succeeded in securing, even at the height of the collectivization crisis, a minimum of basic supplies sufficient to keep the urban economy going, and to maintain the volume of foreign trade at an all-time post-1917 peak. On this basis additional techniques of dealing with inflation were developed, which aimed either at mopping up the excessive demand or at stimulating output, and which varied as to their nature and relative importance depending on the circumstances. But more significant than all these variations was the fundamental fact that the ever-present goods famine ceased now to be a source of danger which might culminate in peasant supply strikes and in political upheaval. It became a price willingly paid for the possibility of letting investment soar both in volume and in depth beyond the boldest dreams of yesterday's "superindustrializers." The need for a substantial increase in the supply of consumers goods within a few years, which had loomed so large in Preobrazhenski's argument, no longer seemed important either as a major objective or as a limiting factor of industrialization: The "minimum of wants" could be asked to wait a little longer.

It was only logical that the author of the theory of "primitive socialist accumulation" was ambivalent in his attitude toward the new realities. Indeed, the story of Preobrazhenski's attempts to adapt himself to the "general line" is sufficiently revealing to warrant a brief digression. In 1929 he broke with Trotsky and gave up his opposition to the official policy, in the sincere belief that the First Five Year Plan constituted a victory for his ideas. Yet in 1930 he was reported to be aghast at the ruthlessness with which grain exports were pressed forward against peasant resistance, and to predict that this would lead to civil war.[10] In the following year he summed up his views in an article "O metodologii sostavleniya genplana i vtoroi pyatiletki" (On the Methodology of Construction of the General Plan and the Second Five Year Plan) and submitted it to the leading economic periodical *Problemy ekonomiki*. The article was never printed but its main ideas can be gauged from the scathing attacks upon it which appeared soon afterward [11] and which fortunately contained extensive quotations. One can gather from these excerpts that Preobrazhenski began by emphasizing the need for rapid expansion during the reconstruction period as dictated by the necessity "to liquidate the class division of society and to reequip technologically the whole labor force of society on the technical level, say, of 1930–1931 during the next five or six years." According to his assumption, 54 million working people out of a total of 60 million had to undergo such reequipment. The reason for speed lay "in the increased danger of intervention and blockade." This sounded like a sweeping endorsement of the official policy at that time.

The sequel, however, was in a different vein. He prepared a scheme designed to show that, other things being equal, the tempo of growth in output would be several times higher in a situation of unused capacity reserves than in cases where additional equipment had to be constructed first. He stressed that the required reequipment was impossible without an intensified accumulation at the expense of consumption, and indicated that this was what actually had happened during the first three years of the Five Year Plan. He concluded this analysis (which drew loud cries of indignation) by applying his acceleration-like concept in reverse, and by predicting that a large part of the capacity in the investment-goods industry which was geared to the reequipment of the whole economy at a terrific rate of speed, would become redundant as the reequipment approached completion. A sharp increase in the share of consumption in the national income, accompanied possibly by some public works, would then become imperative in order to avoid the "overaccumulation crisis."

The last part of the argument, while logically coherent, was unrealistic: there was no "overbuilding" in Soviet investment industries toward the end of the First Five Year Plan, not in the least because it was patently impossible to reequip 54 out of 60 million people on the basis of up-to-date technology within five or six years. But Preobrazhenski's opponents had no objections whatsoever on this particular score. It was the idea that the astronomic rate of growth implied in such "reequipment" could not continue forever which aroused their ire.

◻

The basic "autonomous" inducements to invest could now assert themselves freely. They reflected two basic characteristics in the men of the "Stalin epoch" — a sense of irreducible bipolarity in the world coupled with a supreme readiness to eradicate everything that cannot be effectively controlled. The extent of military preparedness had to be sufficient not merely to fight off an attack or to make the Soviet state sufficiently strong in order (as Stalin put it as early as 1925) "to come out last" in case of an intracapitalist war and "to throw our decisive weight on the scales, the weight that will tip the scales." [12] It had to secure, with the same crushing degree of finality, the destruction of the enemy, superiority over temporary allies, and domination over followers all over the globe. That the same rules of total warfare fully applied to the domestic scene, is clear from all the foregoing; in fact, it was here that the decisive showdown had to take place at a much earlier stage of the game. The rapid-fire industrialization and the sweeping collectivization were not merely devices of economic policy, but means of extending the direct control of the totalitarian state over the largest possible number within the shortest time. Yet the way in which this extension was brought about had, from the viewpoint of the "controllers," a high value of its own. The lightning speed of the drive pulverized the will to resist. It whipped into enthusiastic action millions of young people yearning for heroic adventure. Last but not least, it succeeded in producing among many former stalwarts of the various intraparty oppositions the feeling that what had occurred was too far-reaching to be reversed without wrecking the whole social setup born of the revolution and that the thing

to do under the circumstances was not to "rock the boat"
but to close ranks in order to minimize the risks involved in
the adopted policies.

It was this unique blend of creeping fear, exhilaration of
battle, and *la-patrie-en-danger* psychosis that provided the
intellectual climate for Stalin's "revolution from above." In
such a climate there was no room for the ideas and concepts
which have been presented on the pages of this study. We
have seen the men who had defended them to be far apart in
their initial blueprints, and even more — in the political
premises on which these blueprints were based. But all of
them — Left, Right, or Center — operated under the assumption that in the sphere of economic policy there are
resistances of material which call not for a smashing knock-
out blow but for some kind of coexistence of heterogeneous
socio-economic setups for a long time to come, with the
result of an uneasy compromise shifting only gradually in the
desired direction. They were more than once swayed in their
reasoning by the emotions of political battle, in which quarter was neither asked nor given. Yet their basic ideas, as
different from the occasional twists in their argument, reflected not the "ideological" juggling of facts and theoretical
concepts but a genuine effort to come to grips with complex
and intractable realities and to make the eventual solutions
stand up against criticism. True, most of the participants in
the great debate had been intellectually formed in the ranks
of the Bolshevik old guard, which represented in the prerevolutionary period the authoritarian wing of Russian
Marxism. But none of them succeeded any more than Lenin
himself did in carrying through to its Stalinist perfection the
basic attitudes toward man and society inherent in the elitist
conception — the refusal to tolerate spheres of social life
not fully manipulable from above, seeing weakness if not
outright betrayal behind any diversity in thought and action,

and the determination to use every means in order to stamp it out. It was the failure of Bukharin, Preobrazhenski, and others to live up to this totalitarian code that sealed their fate. All of them perished in the purges of the thirties.

Had the above lines appeared in print before March 1953, it might be possible to conclude at this point. Yet even then the picture would be less than complete; from today's vantage point it would appear misleadingly one-sided.

On the basis of the preceding paragraphs the reader might believe that the difficulties with which the men of the twenties had been wrestling faded out of existence after reaching a fever pitch in the early thirties. Yet they did not, and while it would be presumptuous to attempt here an exhaustive analysis of the distortions which the high-pressure industrialization left in the structure of the economy, a quick glance at some of them may be in order. The missing "future bricks" of Bukharin are by no means an anachronism under conditions of uncertainty about the quality and steadiness of supply flows — a situation which prevails wherever the ambitious targets strain capacity to the breaking point and chew up the stocks of intermediate goods. At the same time a variety of adjustments to those shortages which could have been anticipated in advance provides a fitting footnote to Bazarov's strictures against "superficial industrial expansion." The limitations of capacity together with the injunction to expand it in the greatest possible hurry lead to neglect of maintenance and repair of existing plant, encourage production and use of inferior material in relatively large quantities, and impel the planners to keep on a short investment ration such highly capital-using items of social overheads as housing and transportation. The "dual economy" approach, officially scorned and rejected, moves in through the back door, as it were, and asserts itself in the coexistence of advanced and backward methods in the interrelated industries or even in various departments of the same production units. But a shortage-ridden economy is not merely using to the hilt old and obsolete machinery alongside with the new at each particular moment of time; it is not infrequently inhibited in shifting to the production of newer models as long as this would require a costly and time-consuming reconstruction of the equipment-producing plant. Last but by no means least, the Soviet society, after a quarter of a century of unparalleled industrial and urban development had to live on a lower-quality per capita diet than at the time when it was, to a very large extent, a society of wretchedly poor peasants — a fact which, for obvious reasons, was deeply disturbing not merely from the viewpoint of consumers' welfare.

There could hardly be a doubt that the increase in social productivity imputable to a value unit of newly-installed plant would under such circumstances be smaller than in case of a slower expansion — much more so, one might add, than would follow from the standard assumption that the marginal efficiency of investment tends to decline as the rate of investment increases. Indeed, it is not inconceivable that at some later point of time a development pattern entailing a smaller but more balanced and more selectively organized volume of investment could have overtaken the Stalinist method — provided that the rate of investment in this moderate pattern would still be large, by usual standards of comparison, and that it would allow for significant economies of scale. Bukharin's warning that "the overextension of capital expenditure . . . will eventually retard the tempo of development" would then have come true in the long run.* Yet the planners of the Stalin era ignored such pos-

---

* To mention just two examples: it would not be impossible for the Stalin-type economy to slow down, after the initial period of rapid-fire growth, as compared with what one might call the "advanced-Bukharin-

sibilities not only because their strategy demanded a maximum economic potential at an earlier date (a point which,
paradoxically enough, the archmoderate Shanin anticipated
more clearly than others), but also because the backlogs
encountered in our earlier discussion would act as effective
shock absorbers. The overhang of agricultural excess population permitted the manning of equipment which was phys-
ically usable with the "surplus" peasants of yesterday
who could be removed from the countryside without a
notable detriment to agricultural output and be employed
at a real wage barely exceeding their wretchedly low consumption levels of the earlier status. The yawning gap in
efficiency between the huge blocks of rundown and obsolete

---

type" economy because (1) the undermaintenance and inferior quality of
a large part of its equipment would cause the "replacement echo" to come
earlier, and (2) the neglect of transportation which was a source of
continual strain and gave a wrong slant to the locational policy would have
to be made good eventually at the price of massive diversion of investment
from "quicker" uses. (On the other hand, one could visualize a situation
when the economy developing along the Stalinist lines is hit by important
inventions which require a certain minimum of steel-producing capacity
for their extensive application. In such a case, one might argue, the
circumstance that the economy in question, owing to the policy of maximizing its growth during the early period, has this necessary minimum at its
command, permits it to take a big forward leap; and this could tilt the scales
against the moderate pattern. The decisive point is whether or not the
differences in volumes of investment and, more particularly, in steel-producing capacity would be large enough to make it impossible for the
Bukharin-type economy to avail itself of the great opportunity — a question
which obviously cannot be decided *a priori*.) The whole argument, it goes
without saying, is seriously incomplete at least in two respects: (1) it is
based on the assumption that voluntary time-preferences of the population
can be not only overruled but entirely disregarded — a premise which is
fairly stiff to operate on, even for totalitarian planners; and (2) it fails
to consider the allocative inefficiencies inherent in the system of top-heavy
centralized planning which is clearly not unrelated to the exigencies of the
adopted pattern of growth without being fully attributable to them. It
should be equally plain finally, that the standard Marxian model, even
in its more refined Fel'dman version, would be of little help to resolve
the issues at hand: its rigid "fixed-coefficients" assumptions would be ill-
designed to cope with the situation of an economy which has been forced
to grow at a rate far exceeding its potentialities and, more specifically,
heavily overtaxing the capacity of its capital-goods sector.

Russian machinery and the up-to-date Western models made it possible to achieve considerable forward strides in productivity in spite of the slapdash way in which investment decisions were made and carried out — particularly when new technology could cooperate with newly-opened natural resources and with labor whose social opportunity cost was exceedingly low. The powerful expansion of railroad network under the Tsars, finally, made it easier for their successors to forego a large scale investment into the bulkiest type of "social overheads" at the start of the industrialization drive.

But the situation of the twenties has repeated itself "on a higher level," to use a favorite Soviet term; the industrialization drive which had owed much of its dazzling successes to the existence of the backlogs ran into difficulties after having filled the empty spaces to the brims. Manpower to operate the industrial plant was no longer available *ad lib.* Demand for food on the part of growing cities could no longer be satisfied without substantial investment in agriculture. Transportation has developed into a formidable bottleneck straining the economy and threatening to distort very seriously the locational pattern. No doubt, the capacity of the Soviet capital-goods industry has grown tremendously in the meantime. But the demands for its services have also gone up. Mechanized agriculture claims much larger current inputs than during the First Five Year Plan (not to speak of the pre-1928 stage); armament production is rapidly growing in importance; and it is more than risky to repeat the performance of the initial years when imports of foreign equipment amounting in some crucial lines to more than half of the apparent consumption were paid for by record-breaking exports of grain while famine was stalking the country. Moreover, foreign developments are also much less propitious. The West is showing a good deal more economic stability and international cohesion than in the interwar period. The advent of the nuclear age has power-

fully added to the pressure on capital resources and set a
much higher risk premium on "throwing the decisive weight
into the scales." Huge claims of the new ally, Communist
China, can be ignored only at grave peril. The emphasis
in the "who-whom?" contest has had therefore to shift from
the dramatic breakthrough to the long pull requiring the
rational husbanding of available means. And just at the
point when droves of chickens started coming home to
roost, the chief architect of the system departed from the
scene, leaving behind a document in which lip service to
"economic laws" was coupled with renewed emphasis on
priority for heavy industry, and the insistence that capitalism
was more decadent than ever.[13]

Stalin seemed confident to the end that he could shrug off
the mounting difficulties. His successors no longer share this
sanguine view. They are, as a leading Western analyst of
Soviet developments put it not long ago, "confronted with
Bukharin's problem in a new guise,"[14] and they know it.
The years which have elapsed since March 1953 have witnessed persistent attempts to grapple with stubborn realities
by reducing glaring disproportions and by loosening-up
institutional rigidities in order to impart to the system a
larger measure of balance, suppleness, and flexibility. But not
only the great issues of the twenties are now back in the
forefront; the memories of men who raised them are being
resurrected from oblivion by the standard bearers of a new
heresy, who do not want reforms but a reformation. Wolf-
gang Harich, the rebellious theoretician of East German
Communism, cites "the thoughts of Trotsky and even more
of Bukharin" as the sources of his inspiration. The writers
of the *Poprostu* group which spearheaded the "Polish
October" enthusiastically praise Bukharin, with a leading
agricultural expert of the ruling party expressing qualified
assent. The martyr of Communist "revisionism," Imre Nagy,
writing only several months before the Hungarian revolu-

tion, solemnly quotes Stalin in support of his views — but the Stalin of 1926 and 1927 when the future promoter of the Five Year Plans was still foursquare "for Bukharin." And, as we move from the shaky periphery to the sturdier center, Khrushchev is certainly not distorting things too much when in an angry blast he pins the label of Bukharinism on the Soviet economists who dared, in the heyday of the Malenkov era, to challenge the dogma of preponderant growth of heavy industry as a *conditio sine qua non* of economic progress. There is certainly no going back to the late twenties. But it is equally incontrovertible that ideas which reverberated through the Soviet Union three decades ago and which since then have been blackened, denigrated, and proclaimed dead time and time again are now playing their part in one of the most significant developments of our time.

Chronology of Key Events,
1921–1929

	a period of rapid increase in their prices in relation to prices of agricultural products.
October 8	Trotsky, in a letter to the Central Committee, castigates the policy of the arbitrary price reductions and "secretarial bureaucratism"; beginning of his open break with Stalin.
October 15	A declaration, signed by forty-six prominent left-wing Communists headed by Preobrazhenski, strongly criticizes the economic and general policies of the party; strong similarities to Trotsky's position evident.
October 23–24	German Communist uprising in Hamburg ends in failure.

1924

January 16–18	Thirteenth Communist Party Conference: leftist opposition, led by Preobrazhenski and Pyatakov, attacks the policy of lowering industrial prices and calls for accelerated industrialization; adopted resolution denounces Trotskyism as a "petty bourgeois deviation."
January 21	Lenin dies.
May 23–31	Thirteenth Communist Party Congress: on its eve, Central Committee and senior delegates hear Lenin's will calling for Stalin's removal from the General Secretariat; resolution of the Thirteenth Conference condemning Trotskyism is reaffirmed.
August	A short-lived uprising in Georgia, viewed by the official party leadership as a symptom of growing peasant discontent.

1925

April 23–30	Plenary session of the Central Committee: resolution on agricultural policy drafted by Bukharin approves the lifting of restrictions on hiring farm labor and on the leasing of land; reduction in total amount of agricultural tax and greater exemption for poorest peasants favored.

Autumn–Winter	The "goods famine" (repressed inflation).
December 18–31	Fourteenth Communist Party Congress: industrialization oriented toward economic independence proclaimed as the major task; Stalin repudiates Bukharin's "get rich" formula, but defends moderate agricultural policies against the "Leningrad opposition" led by his former associates, Kamenev and Zinov'ev.

1926

October 26–November 3	Fifteenth Communist Party Conference: Stalin and Bukharin in all-out attack against the "oppositionist bloc" headed by Trotsky, Kamenev, and Zinov'ev; policies of the opposition denounced as "social-democratic deviationism" and as a grave threat to the workers-peasant alliance.

1927

April 12	Anti-Communist coup by Chiang Kai-shek in Shanghai; thousands of Communists executed.
November–December	Grain collections drop to less than a half of their level of the last two months of 1926; industrial "goods famine" reappears.
December 2–19	Fifteenth Communist Party Congress: the whole leadership of the left-wing opposition expelled from the party; general directives for the future Five Year Plan emphasize the need for speed as well as for balance, and urge greater support for collective farming.

1928

Spring	Grain collections decline again after temporary improvement during the first three months of the year.
July 4–12	Plenary session of the Central Committee: resolution adopted emphasizes collectivization as the long-range solution, but warns against continued reliance on

compulsory emergency measures, and calls for increases in the price of grain as well as in supplies of industrial goods to the grain producing areas; first signs of the rift between Stalin and the Bukharin-Rykov group.

October
The First Five Year Plan, based on the latest and most ambitious alternative draft, is launched; the grain collection crisis continues unabated.

November 16–24
Plenary session of the Central Committee: "rightist deviation" denounced as chief danger.

1929

January 22
Trotsky gets deportation order; starts journey to Constantinople.

April 16–23
Joint plenary session of the Central Committee and of the Central Control Commission: Stalin openly breaks with Bukharin and Rykov and identifies them and Tomski as leaders of the "rightist deviation"; Bukharin removed as head of the Communist International and as editor of *Pravda*, Tomski — as head of the trade unions.

April 23–29
Sixteenth Communist Party Conference: First Five Year Plan formally ratified; Bukharin group denounced.

Autumn
All-out collectivization drive begins.

Bibliography of Sources Cited
References
Index

Bibliography of Sources Cited

M. Barun, "Vozrast i iznoshennost' osnovnogo kapitala promy-shlennosti" (Age and Wear and Tear of the Fixed Capital of the Industry). *Sotsialisticheskoe khozyaistvo* (Socialist Economy), 1928, no. 1.

F. M. Bator, "On Capital Productivity, Input Allocation and Growth," *QJE*, 71, February 1957.

V. A. Bazarov, "Itogi istekshego goda i zloba tekushchego dnya" (Balance Sheet of the Last Year and the Worries of Today), *EO*, December 1925.

———— "O metodologii postroeniya perspektivnykh planov" (On the Methodology of Construction of the Perspective Plans), *PKh*, July 1926.

———— "Perspektivy 1926/27 ekonomicheskogo goda" (Perspectives of the Economic Year 1926/27), *EO*, September 1926.

———— *Kapitalisticheskie tsikly i vosstanovitel'ny protsess khozyaistva SSSR* (Capitalist Cycles and the Process of Restoration of the USSR), Moscow-Leningrad, 1927.

————"O nashikh khozyaistvennykh perspektivakh i perspektivnykh planakh" (On Our Economic Perspectives and Perspective Plans), *EO*, May 1927.

———— "Printsipy postroeniya perspektivnykh planov" (Principles for Construction of the Perspective Plans), *PKh*, February 1928.

———— "O perspektivakh khozyaistvennogo i kul'turnogo razvitiya" (On the Perspectives of the Economic and Cultural Development), *EO*, June 1928.

A. Bergson, "The Russian Economy Since Stalin," *Foreign Affairs 34*, January 1956.

N. S. Buchanan, *International Investment and Domestic Welfare*, New York, 1945.

N. I. Bukharin, *Ekonomika perekhodnogo perioda* (Economy of the Transition Period), Moscow, 1920.

———— "Khozyaistvenny rost i problema raboche-krest'yanskogo bloka" (The Economic Growth and the Problem of the Workers-Peasant Bloc), *B*, November 5, 1924.

———— "Novoe otkrovenie o sovetskoi ekonomike ili kak mozhno pogubit' raboche-krest'yanski blok" (New Revelation of the

Soviet Economy or How Can the Workers-Peasant Bloc Be Destroyed), *B*, December 10, 1924.

——— "K kritike ekonomicheskoi platformy oppozitsii" (Critique of the Economic Program of the Opposition), *B*, January 15, 1925.

——— "O novoi ekonomicheskoi politike i nashikh zadachakh" (On the New Economic Policy and Our Tasks), *B*, April 30 and June 1, 1925.

——— *K voprosu o trotskizme* (On Trotskyism), Moscow-Leningrad, 1925.

——— *Building Up Socialism*, London, 1926.

——— *Mezhdunarodnoe i vnutrennee polozhenie; doklad na XV konferentsii Moskovskogo raiona VKP (b)* International and Domestic Situation; Report to the XV Conference of the Moscow Region of the CPSU [b]). Moscow, 1927.

——— "K desyatiletiyu Oktyabr'skoi revolyutsii" (To the Tenth Anniversary of the October Revolution), *P*, October 16 and 18, 1927.

——— "Ob itogakh ob'edinennogo plenuma TsK and TsKK VKP(b)" (On the Results of the Joint Plenum of the Central Committee and the Central Control Commission of the CPSU [b]), *P*, November 4, 1927.

——— Report to the XVI Moscow Regional Conference of the CPSU (b), *P*, November 23 and 24, 1927.

——— "Uroki khebozagotovok, shakhtinskogo dela i zadachi partii" (Lessons of the Grain Collections and of the Shakhty Case, and the Tasks of the Party), *P*, April 19, 1928.

——— "Zametki ekonomista" (Notes of an Economist), *P*, September 30, 1928.

——— *Imperializm i nakoplenie kapitala* (Imperialism and Accumulation of Capital), 4 ed., Moscow-Leningrad, 1929.

K. Butayev, "K voprosu o material'noi baze sotsializma" (On the Problem of the Material Basis of Socialism), *Problemy ekonomiki* (Problems of Economy), 1932, no. 1.

E. Dahmen, "Technology, Innovation, and International Industrial Transformation," in L. H. Dupriez, ed., *Economic Progress*, Louvain, 1955.

M. H. Dobb, *Political Economy and Capitalism*, New York, 1945.

——— *Soviet Economic Development since 1917*, New York, 1948.

E. D. Domar, *Essays in the Theory of Economic Growth*, New York, 1957.

R. S. Eckaus, "The Factor Proportions Problem in Underdeveloped Areas," *American Economic Review 45*, September 1955.

G. A. Fel'dman, "K teorii tempov narodnogo dokhoda" (On the Theory of the Rate of Growth of the National Income), *PKh*, November and December, 1928.

A. Gerschenkron, "The Soviet Indices of Industrial Production," *Review of Economic Statistics* 29, November 1947.

────── "Economic Backwardness in Historical Perspective," in B. F. Hoselitz, ed., *The Progress of Underdeveloped Areas*, Chicago, 1952.

────── "The Problem of Economic Development in Russian Intellectual History of the Nineteenth Century," in E. J. Simmons, ed., *Continuity and Change in Russian and Soviet Thought*, Cambridge, Mass., 1955.

Gosplan SSSR, *Kontrol'nye tsifry narodnogo khozyaistva SSSR na 1926/27 god* (Control Figures of the National Economy of the USSR for 1926/27), Moscow, 1926.

V. G. Groman, "O nekotorykh zakonomernostyakh empiricheski obnaruzhivaemykh v nashem narodnom khozyaistve" (On Certain Regularities to be Empirically Observed in Our National Economy), *PKh*, January 1925.

B. A. Gukhman, "Dinamika promyshlennosti Rossii v svyazi s dinamikoi narodnogo khozyaistva" (Dynamics of Russia's Industry in Connection with the Dynamics of the National Economy), in E. I. Kviring, S. P. Sereda, A. M. Ginzburg, eds., *Promyshlennost' i narodnoe khozyaistvo, sbornik statei* (Industry and National Economy, Collection of Articles), Moscow, 1927.

────── "Na rubezhe" (At the Divide), *PKh*, August 1928.

J. R. Hicks, *The Theory of Wages*, London, 1932.

────── "World Recovery After War — A Theoretical Analysis," *Economic Journal* 57, June 1947.

"Iz pis'ma ssyl'nogo oppozitsionera" (From a Letter of an Exiled Oppositionist), *Byulleten' oppozitsii (bol'shevikov-lenintsev)* Bulletin of The Opposition (of Bolsheviks-Leninists), March 1931.

A. E. Kahn, "Investment Criteria in Development Programs," *QJE*, 65, February 1951.

G. Krumin, "Osnovnye dostizheniya istekshego khozyaistvennogo goda i blizhaishie zadachi" (Basic Achievements of the Past Economic Year and Immediate Tasks), *EO*, December 1925.

V. I. Lenin, *Sochineniya* (Collected Works), 38 vols.; 4 ed.; Moscow, 1941–1958.

────── *Selected Works in Two Volumes*, Moscow, 1950–1952.

────── "Zamechaniya na knigu N. I. Bukharina: 'Ekonomika perekhodnogo perioda'" (Comments on N. I. Bukharin's book, "Economy of the Period of Transition"), in N. I. Bukharin, V. M. Molotov, M. A. Savel'ev, eds. *Leninski sbornik* (Lenin Collection) XI, Moscow, 1929.

A. P. Lerner, *The Economics of Control*, New York, 1944.

W. A. Lewis, "Economic Development with Unlimited Supplies of Labour," *Manchester School*, 22, May 1954.

———— "Unlimited Labour: Further Notes," *Manchester School,* 26, January 1958.

R. Luxemburg, *The Accumulation of Capital,* New Haven, 1951.

P. I. Lyashchenko, *History of the National Economy of the USSR to the 1917 Revolution,* New York, 1949.

D. Maretski, "Khozyaistvennaya platforma ob'edinennoi oppozitsii" (Economic Program of the United Opposition), *B,* September 30, 1926.

K. Marx, *Capital,* 3 vols., Chicago, 1903–1909.

———— *Theories of Surplus Value,* New York, 1952.

M. Mekler, "Obshchi krizis kapitalizma i bor'ba dvukh sistem v svete teorii Preobrazhenskogo" (General Crisis of Capitalism and the Struggle of Two Systems in the Light of Preobrazhenski's Theory), in Kommunisticheskaya Akademiya, Institut mirovogo khozyaistva i mirovoi politiki, *Zakat kapitalizma v trotskistskom zerkale (o knige E. Preobrazhenskogo "Zakat kapitalizma"),* (Communist Academy, Institute of World Economics and World Politics, Decline of Capitalism in the Trotskyite Mirror [on E. Preobrazhenski's book "Decline of Capitalism"]), Moscow, 1932.

V. Motylev, *Problema tempa razvitiya SSSR* (Problem of the Tempo of Development of the USSR), 3 ed., Moscow, 1929.

R. Nurkse, *Problems of Capital Formation in Underdeveloped Countries,* New York, 1953.

N. P. Oganovski, "Promyshlennost' i sel'skoe khozyaistvo" (Industry and Agriculture), in E. I. Kviring, S. P. Sereda and A. M. Ginzburg, eds. *Promyshlennost' i narodnoe khozyaistvo, sbornik statei* (Industry and National Economy, Collection of Articles), Moscow, 1927.

"Perspektivy khozyaistvennogo razvitiya SSSR (Kontrol'nye tsifry Gosplana)" [Perspectives of the Economic Development of the USSR (Control Figures of the Gosplan)], discussion at the Communist Academy, *VKA,* XVII, 1926.

J. J. Polak, "Balance of Payments Problems of Countries Reconstructing with the Help of Foreign Loans," *QJE,* 57, February 1943, reprinted in H. S. Ellis and L. A. Metzler, eds., *Readings in the Theory of International Trade,* Philadelphia-Toronto, 1950.

E. A. Preobrazhenski, *Bumazhnye den'gi v epokhu proletarskoi diktatury* (Paper Money in the Epoch of Proletarian Dictatorship), Moscow, 1920.

———— Speech at the XIII Conference of the CPSU, *P,* January 18, 1924.

———— "Ekonomicheskie zametki" (Economic Notes), I, *P,* December 15, 1925; II, *B,* March 31, 1926; III, August 30, 1926.

———— *Novaya ekonomika* (New Economy), 2 ed., Moscow, 1926.

———— [Discussion of Chapter III of *Novaya ekonomika* in the Communist Academy], *VKA*, XV, 1926.

———— "Problema khozyaistvennogo ravnovesiya pri konkretnom kapitalizme i v sovetskoi sisteme" (Problem of the Economic Equilibrium under Conditions of the Concrete Capitalism and in the Soviet System), *VKA*, XVII, 1926.

———— "Khozyaistvennoe ravnovesie pri konkretnom kapitalizme i v sisteme SSSR" (Economic Equilibrium under Conditions of the Concrete Capitalism and in the Soviet System), *VKA*, XVIII, 1926.

———— "Khozyaistvennoe ravnovesie v sisteme SSSR" (Economic Equilibrium in the System of the USSR), *VKA*, XXII, 1927.

———— "Levy kurs v derevne i perspektivy" (Leftist Course in the Countryside and the Perspectives), mimeographed, 1928.

———— *Zakat kapitalizma* (Decline of Capitalism), Leningrad, 1931.

G. L. Pyatakov, "K voprosu o vosproizvodstve osnovnogo kapitala" (On the Question of Reproduction of Fixed Capital), *Torgovo-Promyshlennaya Gazeta* (Trade and Industry Journal), September 30, 1924.

M. Ragol'ski, "O vreditel'skoi teorii planirovaniya Gromana-Bazarova" (On the Wreckers' Planning Theory of Groman-Bazarov), *PKh*, October-November 1930.

J. Robinson, *Collected Economic Essays*, New York, 1951.

P. N. Rosenstein-Rodan, "Problems of Industrialization of Eastern and Southeastern Europe," *Economic Journal,* 53, June-September, 1943.

A. I. Rykov, Report to the 4th Soviet Congress, *P*, April 23, 1927.

———— Report to the X Congress of the Communist Party of Ukraine, *P*, November 25, 1927.

———— "Tekushchi moment i zadachi partii" (The Present Moment and the Tasks of the Party), *P*, July 15, 1928.

S. M. Schwarz, "Populism and Early Russian Marxism on Ways of Economic Development of Russia (the 1880s and the 1890s)" in E. J. Simmons, ed., *Continuity and Change in Russian and Soviet Thought*, Cambridge, Mass., 1955.

T. Scitovsky, "Two Concepts of External Economies," *Journal of Political Economy*, 52, April 1954.

———— "Sur deux principes de maximation du profit et quelques-unes de leurs implications," *Revue Economique*, May, 1955.

A. K. Sen, "Some Notes on the Choice of Capital Intensity in Development Planning," *QJE*, 71, November 1957.

L. Shanin, "Ekonomicheskaya priroda nashego beztovariya" (The Economic Essence of Our Commodity Shortage), *EO*, November 1925.

———— "Voprosy novogo kursa" (Problems of the New Course), *B*, January 30, 1926.

I. V. Stalin, *Sochineniya* (Collected Works), 13 vols., Moscow, 1946–1951.

———— *Economic Problems of Socialism in the USSR*, New York, 1952.

———— (jointly with A. I. Rykov and V. V. Kuibyshev), "O uspekhakh i nedostatkakh kampanii za rezhim ekonomii" (On the Successes and the Shortcomings of the Campaign for the Regime of Economy), *P*, August 17, 1926.

S. G. Strumilin, *Ocherki sovetskoi ekonomiki* (Essays on the Soviet Economy), 2 ed., Moscow-Leningrad, 1930.

———— *Problemy planirovaniya v SSSR* (Problems of Planning in the USSR), Moscow-Leningrad, 1932.

———— *Chernaya metallurgiya v Rossii i SSSR, tekhnicheski progress za 300 let* (Ferrous Metallurgy in Russia and in the USSR, Technological Progress Over 300 Years), Moscow, 1935.

Trotsky, L., *Towards Socialism or Capitalism?*, London, 1926.

Tsentral'noe Statisticheskoe Upravlenie SSSR, Trudy . . . tom XXIX, *Balans narodnogo khozyaistva Soyuza SSR 1923–24 goda* (Central Statistical Administration of the USSR, Studies . . . vol. XXIX, Balance Sheet of the National Economy of the USSR for 1923–24), Moscow, 1926.

———— *Promyshlennost' SSSR, statisticheski sbornik* (Industry of the USSR, Statistical Handbook), Moscow, 1957.

J. Viner, "Cost Curves and Supply Curves," *Zeitschrift fuer National-oekonomie*, III, 1932, reprinted in R. V. Clemence, ed., *Readings in Economic Analysis*, 2 vols., Cambridge, Mass., 1950, vol. II.

A. P. Vinokur and S. N. Bakulin, eds. *Vneshnyaya torgovlya Soyuza Sovetskikh Sotsialisticheskikh Respublik za period 1918–1927/28 gg., statisticheski sbornik* (Foreign Trade of the Union of Soviet Socialist Republics for the Period of 1918–1927/28, Statistical Handbook), Leningrad-Moscow, 1931.

VKP, *XIV s'ezd Vsesoyuznoi Kommunisticheskoi Partii (b), stenografcheski otchet* (Communist Party of the Soviet Union [b], XIV Congress of the Communist Party of the Soviet Union [b], Stenographic Report), Moscow-Leningrad, 1926.

———— *XV konferentsiya Vsesoyuznoi Kommunisticheskoi Partii (b), stenografcheski otchet* (XV Conference of the Communist Party of the Soviet Union [b], Stenographic Report), Moscow-Leningrad, 1927.

———— *XV s'ezd Vsesoyuznoi Kommunisticheskoi Partii (b), stenografcheski otchet* (XV Congress of the Communist Party of the Soviet Union [b], Stenographic Report), Moscow-Leningrad, 1928.

———— *XVII s'ezd Vsesoyuznoi Kommunisticheskoi Partii (b)*, *steno-grafcheski otchet* (XVII Congress of the Communist Party of the Soviet Union [b], Stenographic Report), Moscow-Leningrad, 1934.

A. A. Young, "Increasing Returns and Economic Progress," *Economic Journal*, 38, December 1928, reprinted in R. V. Clemence, ed., *Readings in Economic Analysis*, 2 vols., Cambridge, Mass., 1950, vol. I.

References

Introduction

1. *Sotsialisticheskoe stroitel'stvo SSSR* (Moscow, 1935), p. 3, cited by A. Gerschenkron in "The Soviet Indices of Industrial Production," *Review of Economic Statistics*, 29 (1947), 218.
2. G. Krumin, "Osnovnye dostizheniya istekshego khozyaistvennogo goda i blizhaishie zadachi," *EO* (December 1925), p. 8.
3. Gosplan SSSR, *Kontrol'nye tsifry narodnogo khozyaistva SSSR na 1926/27 god* (Moscow, 1926), p. 314.
4. Krumin, *EO* (December 1925), p. 8.

Chapter I: The "Lenin Revolution" and Its Interpreter

1. V. I. Lenin, *Sochineniya* (4 ed.; Moscow, 1941–1958), XXXIII, 398.
2. V. I. Lenin, *Selected Works in Two Volumes* (Moscow, 1950–1952), vol. II, pt. 2, p. 601.
3. *Ibid.*, pp. 539–544, 553 (italics mine), 555.
4. *Ibid.*, p. 727. The official translation incorrectly uses the stronger term "overtake" rather than "catch up" to render the meaning of the Russian "dogonyat'."
5. *Ibid.*, p. 751.
6. Lenin, *Sochineniya*, XXXIII, 135.
7. Lenin, *Selected Works*, vol. II, pt. 2, pp. 635–637.
8. "O novoi ekonomicheskoi politike i nashikh zadachakh," pt. I, *B* (April 30, 1925), pp. 8–9.
9. N. I. Bukharin, *Imperializm i nakoplenie kapitala* (4 ed.; Moscow-Leningrad, 1929), p. 63.
10. "Khozyaistvenny rost i problema raboche-krest'yanskogo bloka," *B* (November 5, 1924), p. 28.
11. *Ibid.*, p. 29.
12. *Ibid.*, pp. 31–32.
13. "O novoi . . . zadachakh," pt. II, *B* (June 1, 1925), pp. 3–4.
14. *B* (November 5, 1924), p. 34.
15. *B* (June 1, 1925), p. 12.
16. N. I. Bukharin, *K voprosu o trotskizme* (Moscow-Leningrad. 1925), p. 120.

17. Bukharin, *Imperializm*, p. 71.
18. *Ibid.*, pp. 62, 65.
19. *B* (November 5, 1924), p. 27.
20. *Ibid.*, p. 30.
21. "K kritike ekonomicheskoi platformy oppozitsii," *B* (January 15, 1925), p. 56.
22. "Novoe otkrovenie o sovetskoi ekonomike ili kak mozhno pogubit' raboche-krest'yanski blok," *B* (December 10, 1924), p. 33.
23. *B* (April 30, 1925), p. 14.

CHAPTER II: The Challenge from the Right and the Left

1. L. Shanin, "Ekonomicheskaya priroda nashego beztovariya," *EO* (November 1925), pp. 32–33.
2. *Ibid.*, p. 37.
3. "Voprosy novogo kursa," *B* (January 30, 1926), p. 72.
4. *Ibid.*, pp. 70, 71.
5. *Ibid.*, p. 77.
6. *Ibid.*, pp. 77–78.
7. *EO* (November 1925), p. 38.
8. *B* (January 30, 1926), p. 74.
9. *Ibid.*, p. 75.
10. *Ibid.*, pp. 74–75.
11. *EO* (November 1925), pp. 36–37.
12. *Novaya ekonomika* (2 ed.; Moscow, 1926), p. 39.
13. *Ibid.*, p. 131.
14. *Ibid.*, p. 124.
15. "In a year from now, we won't be able to increase the output of our metallurgy by utilizing the equipment of old plants" ("Ekonomicheskie zametki," pt. II, *B* [March 31, 1926], p. 64).
16. "Ekonomicheskie zametki," pt. I, *P* (December 15, 1925).
17. *Ibid.*
18. Speech before the Communist Academy, *VKA*, XVI (1926), p. 231.
19. *Ibid.*, p. 235.
20. "Khozyaistvennoe ravnovesie v sisteme SSSR," *VKA*, XXII (1927).
21. *Ibid.*, p. 69.
22. *Novaya ekonomika*, p. 195.
23. *Ibid.*, p. 279.
24. *VKA*, XXII (1927), p. 69.
25. *Ibid.*, p. 70.
26. *Novaya ekonomika*, p. 231.
27. *Ibid.*, p. 262.
28. *Zakat kapitalizma*, p. 26 n.

29. *VKA*, XXII (1927), p. 42.

30. *Novaya ekonomika*, p. 92.

31. See A. A. Young, "Increasing Returns and Economic Progress," *Economic Journal*, 38 (December 1928), reprinted in the first volume of R. V. Clemence, ed., *Readings in Economic Analysis* (Cambridge, Mass., 1950); P. N. Rosenstein-Rodan, "Problems of Industrialization of Eastern and Southeastern Europe," *Economic Journal*, 43 (June-September 1943); R. Nurkse, *Problems of Capital Formation in Underdeveloped Countries* (New York, 1953).

32. *Novaya ekonomika*, p. 102.

33. *Ibid.*, pp. 145–146.

34. *Ibid.*, p. 150.

35. *Ibid.*, p. 328.

36. *Ibid.*, p. 327.

37. *Ibid.*, p. 183.

38. L. Trotsky, *Towards Socialism or Capitalism?* (London, 1926), p. 89.

39. *Novaya ekonomika*, pp. 183–184.

40. *Ibid.*, p. 45.

41. *Ibid.*, p. 143.

42. *Ibid.*, p. 136.

43. *VKA*, XXII (1927), p. 64.

44. *Ibid.*, p. 123.

45. *P* (January 18, 1924).

46. *Novaya ekonomika*, p. 186 (italics mine).

47. *Ibid.*

48. *Ibid.*, p. 40.

49. *Ibid.*, p. 31.

50. *Ibid.*, pp. 284–286.

51. See Litvinov's speech during the discussion in the Communist Academy, *VKA*, XVII (1926), p. 257.

52. *VKA*, XXII (1927), p. 41.

53. *Zakat kapitalizma*, p. 78.

54. *VKA*, XXII (1927), p. 41.

55. *Novaya ekonomika*, pp. 197, 278.

56. *Ibid.*, p. 224.

57. *Ibid.*, p. 70.

CHAPTER III: Attempt at Synthesis

1. "Perspektivy 1926/27 ekonomicheskogo goda," *EO* (September 1926), p. 6.

2. *Ibid.*, p. 9.

3. "O metodologii postroeniya perspektivnykh planov," *PKh* (July 1926), p. 18.

4. *Kapitalisticheskie tsikly i vosstanovitel'ny protsess khozyaistva SSSR* (Moscow-Leningrad, 1927), pp. 98–99.

5. *PKh* (July 1926), p. 12.

6. "Printsipy postroeniya perspektivnykh planov," *PKh* (February 1928), p. 47.

7. *Ibid.*, p. 63.

8. *PKh* (July 1926), p. 12.

9. "Itogi istekshego goda i zloba tekushchego dnya," *EO* (December 1925), p. 40.

10. *Ibid.*, p. 36.

11. *PKh* (July 1926), pp. 18–19.

12. *PKh* (February 1928), p. 47.

13. *Ibid.*

14. *Ibid.*, pp. 48–49.

15. *Ibid.*, p. 49.

16. *Ibid.*, p. 51.

17. *Ibid.*, p. 52.

18. *Ibid.*, p. 45.

19. "O nashikh khozyaistvennykh perspektivakh i perspektivnykh planakh," *EO* (May 1927), pp. 43–44.

20. *K metodologii perspektivnogo planirovaniya* (1924), p. 8. Quoted from M. Ragol'ski, "O vreditel'skoi teorii planirovaniya Gromana-Bazarova," *PKh* (October-November 1930), p. 75.

21. Report of November 2, 1923, Archive of Gosplan. Quoted by S. G. Strumilin, *Problemy planirovaniya v SSSR* (Moscow-Leningrad, 1932), p. 40.

22. *EO* (May 1927), p. 46.

23. "O perspektivakh khozyaistvennogo i kul'turnogo razvitiya," *EO* (June 1928), p. 64.

24. Speech at the Second Congress of the Planning Agencies in 1927. Quoted by Strumilin, *Problemy*, p. 121.

25. "O nekotorykh zakonomernostyakh empiricheski obnaruzhivaemykh v nashem narodnom khozyaistve," *PKh* (January 1925), p. 94.

26. *Ibid.*, pp. 95, 100.

Chapter IV: A Readjustment of Views

1. "K voprosu o vosproizvodstve osnovnogo kapitala," *Torgovo-promyshlennaya gazeta* (September 30, 1924).

2. "K kritike ekonomicheskoi platformy oppozitsii," *B* (January 15, 1925), p. 56.

3. VKP, *XIV s'ezd* (Moscow-Leningrad, 1926), p. 135.

4. *Mezhdunarodnoye i vnutrennee polozhenie; doklad XV Konferentsii Moskovskogo rayona VKP (b)*, (Moscow, 1927), pp. 38–39.

5. *Building Up Socialism* (London, 1926), pp. 1–2.

6. *P* (April 23, 1927).

7. VKP, *XV s'ezd* (Moscow-Leningrad, 1928), p. 1041.

8. See Chapter II.

9. See D. Maretski, "Khozyaistvennaya programma ob'edinennoi oppozitsii," *B* (September 30, 1926), p. 134.

10. See VKP, *XV konferentsiya* (Moscow-Leningrad, 1927), pp. 113–114.

11. *P* (November 25, 1927).

12. *P* (November 24, 1927).

13. It appeared in *Pravda* on September 30, 1928. For an English translation, see *International Press Correspondence 8* (October 19 and 26, November 2, 1928).

14. *P* (October 18, 1927).

15. A. I. Rykov, "Tekushchi moment i zadachi partii," *P* (July 15, 1928).

16. B. Gukhman, "Dinamika promyshlennosti Rossii v svyazi s dinamikoi narodnogo khozyaistva," in *Promyshlennost' i narodnoe khozyaistvo* (Moscow, 1927), p. 95.

17. VKP, *XV s'ezd* (Moscow-Leningrad, 1928), p. 1297.

18. *Ibid.*, pp. 1295–1296.

19. N. I. Bukharin, "Ob itogakh ob'edinennogo plenuma TsK and TsKK VKP (b)," *P* (November 4, 1927).

20. Rykov, *P* (November 25, 1927).

21. Bukharin, *P* (November 4, 1927).

22. N. I. Bukharin, "Uroki khlebozagotovok, shakhtinskogo dela i zadachi partii," *P* (April 19, 1928).

23. Rykov, *P* (April 27, 1927).

24. Rykov, *P* (July 15, 1928).

25. Rykov, *P* (November 25, 1927).

26. VKP, *XV s'ezd* (Moscow-Leningrad, 1928), p. 774.

CHAPTER V: An Exercise in Evasion

1. *Sochineniya*, VII, 355.

2. *Ibid.*, p. 382.

3. *Ibid.*, p. 153.

4. *Ibid.*, pp. 123, 125.

5. *Ibid.*, p. 29.

6. *Ibid.*, VII, 200.

7. *Ibid.*, p. 131.

8. *Ibid.*, pp. 315–316.

9. Compare Shanin's already quoted article, "Voprosy novogo kursa," *B* (January 30, 1926), where the cited passage from Stalin is given in full.

10. *Sochineniya*, VIII, 120.
11. *Ibid.*, p. 132.
12. *Ibid.*, pp. 122–125.
13. *Ibid.*, p. 287.
14. *Ibid.*, pp. 126–129.
15. *Ibid.*, IX, 196 and joint declaration by Stalin, Rykov, and Kuibyshev, "O uspekhakh i nedostatkakh kampanii za rezhim ekonomii," *P* (August 17, 1926).
16. *Sochineniya*, IX, 120.
17. *Ibid.*, pp. 288, 352–353.
18. *Ibid.*, X, 300.
19. *Ibid.*, pp. 301–302.
20. *Ibid.*, p. 309.
21. *Ibid.*, p. 225.

CHAPTER VI: The Imbalance

1. J. R. Hicks, "World Recovery After War — A Theoretical Analysis," *Economic Journal*, 47 (June 1947), 155 (italics mine). The fact that Professor Hicks represented a rather moderate view in the debate on postwar investment policies in his country underscores the significance of this statement.
2. Preobrazhenski, *Novaya ekonomika*, p. 248.
3. S. G. Strumilin, *Ocherki sovetskoi ekonomiki* (2 ed.; Moscow-Leningrad, 1930), p. 119.
4. Trudy Tsentral'nogo Statisticheskogo Upravleniya, tom XXIX, *Balans narodnogo khozyaistva Soyuza SSR 1923–24 goda* (Moscow, 1926), pt. II, p. 31.
5. *Promyshlennost' SSSR* (Moscow, 1957), p. 107.
6. *Vneshnyaya torgovlya Soyuza Sotsialisticheskikh Sovetskikh Respublik za period 1918–1927/28 gg.* (Moscow-Leningrad, 1931), pp. 16, 30, 40.
7. See M. Barun, "Vozrast i iznoshennost' osnovnogo kapitala promyshlennosti," *Sotsialisticheskoe khozyaistvo* (1928), no. 1, pp. 92, 96.
8. See S. G. Strumilin, *Chernaya metallurgiya v Rossii i SSSR, tekhnicheski progress za 300 let* (Moscow, 1935), p. 282.
9. Abba P. Lerner, *The Economics of Control* (New York, 1944), ch. xxv.
10. See *VKA*, XXII, 66, 77, and *Zakat kaputalizma*, p. 71.
11. *Novaya ekonomika*, p. 282.
12. Bukharin, *B* (January 15, 1925), p. 54.
13. Bukharin, *B* (December 10, 1924), p. 27.

CHAPTER VII: Relaxation Possibilities

1. The rate-of-turnover criterion was defended by J. J. Polak ("Balance of Payments Problems of Countries Reconstructing with the Help of Foreign Loans," *QJE*, 57 [February 1943], reprinted in H. S. Ellis and L. A. Metzler, eds., *Readings in the Theory of International Trade* [Philadelphia-Toronto, 1950]), and N. S. Buchanan (*International Investment and Domestic Welfare* [New York, 1945]). Among numerous articles containing a critique of this point of view, the present writer found the following particularly helpful: A. E. Kahn, "Investment Criteria in Development Programs," *QJE*, 65 (February 1951); F. M. Bator, "On Capital Productivity, Input Allocation, and Growth," *QJE*, 71 (February 1957); A. K. Sen, "Some Notes on the Choice of Capital Intensity in Development Planning," *QJE* (November 1957).

2. See J. Viner, "Cost Curves and Supply Curves," *Zeitschrift fuer Nationaloekonomie*, 3 (1932), reprinted in the second volume of Clemence, ed., *Readings in Economic Analysis;* and T. Scitovsky, "Two Concepts of External Economies," *Journal of Political Economy*, 52 (April 1954).

3. *Novaya ekonomika*, p. 92 (italics mine).

4. *Imperialism, The Highest Stage of Capitalism*, quoted by J. Knapp, "Capital Exports and Growth," *Economic Journal*, 67 (December 1957), 432.

CHAPTER VIII: A Long-Range View

1. See his "Economic Backwardness in Historical Perspective" in B. F. Hoselitz, ed., *The Progress of Underdeveloped Areas* (Chicago, 1952), and his already cited essay "The Problem of Economic Development in Russian Intellectual History of the Nineteenth Century." The discussion of the problem of technological backlog throughout this chapter owes much to Professor Gerschenkron's analysis.

2. *Novaya ekonomika*, p. 207. Very similar statements could be found in Rosa Luxemburg's *Accumulation of Capital*, various writings of Lenin, as well as in the passage from Bukharin quoted on page 19 above.

3. *Ibid.*

4. *VKA*, XVII (1926), 47.

5. *Theories of Surplus Value* (New York, 1952), p. 366.

6. Cf. J. Robinson, "Marx and Keynes" and "Mr. Harrod's Dynamics" in her *Collected Economic Essays* (New York, 1951); also W. A. Lewis, "Economic Development with Unlimited Supplies of Labour," *Manchester School*, 22 (May 1954), and "Unlimited Labour: Further Notes," *Manchester School*, 26 (January 1958).

7. Cf. his paper, "Technology, Innovation, and International Industrial Transformation," in L. H. Dupriez, ed., *Economic Progress* (Louvain, 1955).

8. See Maurice Dobb, *Political Economy and Capitalism* (New York, 1945), p. 286, and T. Scitovsky, "Sur deux principes de maximation du profit et quelques-unes de leurs implications," *Revue Economique* (May 1955), pp. 383–384.

9. Cf. B. A. Gukhman, "Dinamika promyshlennosti Rossii v svyazi s dinamikoi narodnogo khozyaistva," in *Promyshlennost' i narodnoe khozyaistvo* (Moscow, 1927), p. 93.

10. *Promyshlennost' SSR* (Moscow, 1957), p. 106; P. I. Lyashchenko, *History of the National Economy of the USSR* (New York, 1949), p. 672.

11. *Leninski sbornik*, XI (Moscow, 1929), p. 397. The first to call attention to the importance of the "combined development" for the prospects of socialism in Russia was Trotsky who stressed the point shortly after the revolution of 1905.

CHAPTER IX: The Final Decision

1. "Levy kurs v derevne i perspektivy" (mimeographed); available in Trotsky Archives of Houghton Library, Harvard University.

2. *Sochineniya*, XI, 14.

3. *Ibid.*, p. 92.

4. *Ibid.*, XII, 45–47, 92–95.

5. *Ibid.*, XI, 275.

6. *Ibid.*, VIII, 291–292.

7. *Ibid.*, XI, 168.

8. *Ibid.*, XI, 3–4, 235.

9. *Sem'nadtsaty s'ezd Vsesoyuznoi Kommunistcheskoi Partii*, (b) *stenograficheski otchet* (Moscow, 1934), p. 238.

10. "Iz pis'ma ssyl'nogo oppositsionera," *Byulleten' oppozitsii*, March 1931, p. 20.

11. Cf. K. Butayev, "K voprosu o material'noi baze sotsializma," *Problemy ekonomiki*, 1932, no. 1, and M. Mekler, "Obshchi krizis kapitalizma i bor'ba dvukh sistem v svete teorii Preobrazhenskogo," in *Zakat kapitalizma v trotskistkom zerkale* (Moscow, 1932).

12. *Sochineniya*, VII, 14.

13. Joseph Stalin, *Economic Problems of Socialism in the USSR* (New York, 1952).

14. Abram Bergson, "The Russian Economy Since Stalin," *Foreign Affairs*, 34 (January 1956), p. 218. Professor Bergson made this comment in reference to the agricultural situation of the post-Stalin period; yet it could be extended to other aspects of the Soviet economy as well.

Index

Russian Research Center Studies

The Russian Research Center of Harvard University is supported by a grant from the Carnegie Corporation. The Center carries out interdisciplinary study of Russian institutions and behavior and related subjects.

RUSSIAN RESEARCH CENTER STUDIES

* Publications of the Harvard Project on the Soviet Social System.
† Published jointly with the Center for International Affairs, Harvard University.